the cookbook

Karen!
Happy Birthday!
a little bit of
Hawkes Bay flavours
to take with
you 🗴

The Noble Nature
— Ben Jonson

It is not growing like a tree
In bulk, doth make Man better be;
Or standing long an oak, three hundred year,
To fall a log at last, dry, bald, and sere:
    A lily of a day
    Is fairer far in May,
  Although it fall and die that night
  It was the plant and flower of Light.
In small proportions we just beauties see;
And in short measures life may perfect be.

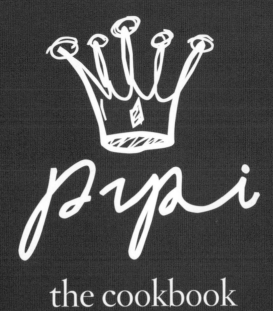

pipi

the cookbook

Recipes by Alexandra Tylee
Photography by Brian Culy

RANDOM HOUSE
NEW ZEALAND

A RANDOM HOUSE BOOK published by Random House New Zealand
18 Poland Road, Glenfield, Auckland, New Zealand

For more information about our titles go to www.randomhouse.co.nz

A catalogue record for this book is available from the National Library
of New Zealand

Random House New Zealand is part of the Random House Group
New York   London   Sydney   Auckland   Delhi   Johannesburg

First published 2012

© 2012 text Alexandra Tylee; photography Brian Culy, except page 11
and 13 Matt Morris and Nathan Hawkes; poems as credited on page xx

The moral rights of the author have been asserted

ISBN 978 1 86979 801 7

Design: Megan van Staden
Printed in Asia by Everbest Printing Co Ltd

For my four sons
Henry Benn, Kodendera Zeus Tylee Ponnapa,
Harry Tylee-Morris and Louis Tylee-Morris.

Also to my husband Chris —
without his help this book could not have been written.

Contents

Introduction 8

Soup 30

Risotto 40

Pasta 50

Pizza 84

Meat 110

Sunday Lunch 142

Fish 150

Vegetables & Salads 168

Bar Food & Drinks 194

Pudding 216

Cakes & Biscuits 250

Children's Birthday
    Parties 266

Extras 284

Poems 298

Acknowledgements 311

Index 314

Introduction

The whole process of Pipi, looking back from where I am now, has been about grief, friends, family and food. About creating a fairy story.

After my second marriage broke down, I fled to Sydney. I am not sure what I was thinking but it seemed like a good idea at the time. Looking back, I do not think I was present when I made that decision. A year before, my second husband and I had lost a son, Zeus, when he was three months old. I don't think I really had had time to deal with this, as we had a very demanding coffee business which was going through a growth period. And as a result a huge part of me just shut down, or floated off to be with Zeus. So going to Sydney was not really thought through.

But once there, I had to get a job. Having not worked for anyone else for a long period of time, since leaving university with a highly enjoyable but not particularly useful classics degree, my only option was to work for myself. So I took over the Woollahra antique centre café. Working there was the beginning of my healing process; it was quiet, but the dealers were wonderful, colourful and very comforting. I had a lot of time to think, maybe too much. So when the opportunity came up to take over the café in the Berkelouw bookshop on Oxford Street in Paddington, I took it, leaving a friend to run the Woollahra one.

I love to cook; it is very creative and immediately satisfying. And exciting; there is always something coming into season to look forward to. I cook with my heart and instinctively. I have had no formal cooking training, rather lots of practice. Beginning with the farm I grew up on, there were always lots of people to feed: shepherds and also smoko for the shearers. Just keeping the tins full was quite a job. After making my way through all my mother's recipes, I discovered a copy of *Mrs Beeton's* and was delighted to find that if you followed her instructions carefully you could make anything, from croissants to soufflés. I think this is one of the main things that gave me the confidence to believe I could cook for a living. And then, later, after coming back from living overseas for three years with my first husband, pregnant with my first child, Henry, we ended up in Carterton. He was the dentist and I was the dentist's wife. Feeling rather tired and with not much else to do, I read recipe books and cooked.

The café in Sydney needed a name. I wanted one that captured the magic that can happen in restaurants, espresso bars and cafés. That moment when a collection of very different people, music, food, light and so on come together and it is perfect for as long as you are drinking your coffee. I was flicking through a cookbook and saw the word 'pipi', and suddenly that was it, that was that moment. I was running on a wild beach in the Wairarapa and when I looked up I saw my son Zeus on the veranda of the bach we were staying in, and when I looked down the whole beach was covered in pipis. So that was it: Pipi.

Pipi has come to have a personality of her own, defiantly female, at times she feels like my subconscious coming to life. In Sydney, if someone burnt the toast it was Pipi's fault. Because we were in a bookshop, a lot of people thought she was Pippi Longstocking, especially when she stomped. But for me, most of the time, she is like a rather stroppy sister: a lot of fun, slightly mad and very demanding.

The café in the bookshop was quite different to Pipi as it is now, but it was the first Pipi and just the beginning. It was open from 10 a.m. until about 10.30 p.m. When I took over they were buying in most of the food, and there was not a proper kitchen. The owners of the bookshop allowed me to convert their wee staff kitchen on the top floor into my prep kitchen. The bookshop sold new books on the ground floor, second-hand on the second and rare ones on the third.

Every morning, at about 6 a.m., I let myself into the bookshop (no one else got there until much later), climbed up the stairs and started cooking. Being around those old books made it seem quite surreal and wonderfully magical. I love books and studied literature at university; I used to imagine the great Greek philosophers were there next to me, helping me make the scones. This was very comforting as I was very much alone. One minute I

had a family and friends and a business in Wellington, then suddenly I was by myself in the middle of a foreign city. Cooking in front of a wee window, which looked down on the gardens of some terrace houses, I used to imagine the breeze that came through it came straight from home.

I frantically made salads, scones, frittatas, cakes, muffins, etc. till 10 a.m., when I took it all downstairs to the café and worked there with help until about 5 or 6 p.m. Many of the people who worked in the bookshop and for me in the café sowed the seeds of what Pipi is today: Massimo the loud Italian, Nathan the art student who later worked for me in New Zealand. With their idiosyncrasies and personalities, they have all contributed in one way or another. Pipi Sydney was all about magic, books and coffee.

When someone very close to you dies, everyone swamps you with good advice, none of which I took. And also lots of well-intentioned clichés: 'You will get over it', 'Time will heal'. Well, it did not. Instead, over the years, I have found a way to live with Zeus dying but I have never accepted it, rather I have grown around his death. It is there inside me and he is here in most things I do. For a long time I just made myself so busy and tired, I had no time to think. This worked for a while but eventually I had to stop. But in Australia, I was in full flight.

As well as keeping myself busy, for those first few years I was still in shock — it was like Zeus's death had not really sunk in. Then one afternoon, while I was in Sydney, I woke up. I suddenly began to feel, and it was unbearable. I woke up and realised I had not only lost Zeus but also my son Henry from my first marriage. When I came to Sydney I had always thought he would too, but of course this did not happen. So after I realised this, it was just a matter of time before I packed all my belongings into a container and flew back to New Zealand to be near Henry.

My plan was to finish the law degree I had started some years before, so I enrolled in the law school at Victoria University in Wellington. As part of the process of selling my share of the coffee business, there was a caveat which did not allow me to own or work in a food or coffee business in Wellington, which I thought I might need to do. So I rented a house in Martinborough, so I could also work, and caught the train to Wellington every morning.

Henry was at a private prep school at the time and I soon realised that I was going to have to come up with a plan to pay for his fees. So I bought a villa on the main street in Greytown, opposite the library. The plan was to just open up the front and sell coffee and biscuits. But I got rather carried away and converted the whole downstairs into a café with a full kitchen, while still living upstairs in the two bedrooms and sharing my bathroom

with the café. This suited me perfectly: the café opened at 7 a.m. and closed at 10 p.m. Again, there was very little time to think. During the process of turning the house into a café and still trying to study, I began to find it hard to remember everything I needed to. When I went to my GP, he pointed out that the human brain can only take so much and trying to cram the rest of my law degree into two years and opening a café on my own was possibly too much. One had to go, and for the second time I stopped studying law so I could focus on a business.

I filled the café with my furniture and Henry, and finally opened at 4 o'clock one Friday night, and none of us have had a moment's peace since.

Pipi Greytown was all about the fire and sofa in the front room, the people, the pizza and the old roses, which my father had moved from our farm when he sold it. Sitting on the sofa out the front of the restaurant for hours after it was closed for the night, watching the milk tankers going by. Wonderful musicians who had been in bands like Blerta who came every Wednesday night and jammed in our front room. The night my friend Melissa and I lost some pizzas down the back of the oven. Playing the hits from the 70s and 80s too loudly and often on repeat. Greytown feels like it is in a paddock — it is very rural and the mountains are visible from everywhere.

One of the big things for me when Zeus died was a very strong feeling that I still needed to look after him. With Pipi in Greytown, I was able to put all the love and nurturing energy which I wanted to give him into our customers and the food. And in return Pipi and her customers nurtured me back to some sort of normality. Zeus had colic for most of his life; he demand-fed almost every two hours. So he and I had a rather odd routine, which I was very loathe to let go of when he died. Not sleeping meant I was close to him. But slowly, as I unwound or was unwound by the people I met in Greytown, I began to sleep.

So that's it, that is the reason for Pipi's existence.

The menu there was a much simpler version of what we do now, mainly pizza and some pasta dishes. And during the day we had an all-day breakfast menu, with counter food, salads, cakes and scones. Coffee was also obviously important.

When I had been in Greytown for about three years, Chris, the manager of the hotel over the road, came in one day wanting to borrow some sugar. Within a few months we were married and pregnant. Luckily I was able to keep working right up until the night before Harry was born, and then, after he arrived, Chris left his job at the White Swan to help us out at Pipi. Chris and I complement each other very well; he has managed and worked in lots of restaurants and was able to harness some of Pipi's wild ways. At times it was rather frantic having a new baby, but living upstairs made it possible. Harry did spend quite a lot of time asleep in his papoose on one of the shelves behind the counter.

Still, when someone approached us wanting to buy the building it got us thinking, and even though that fell through it prompted me to ring a real estate agent in Hawke's Bay to ask if there were any premises suitable to lease for a restaurant. I did not hear anything for ages and then one day he rang and said there was an old fish and chip shop available in Havelock North. The building he was talking about was the one building in the whole of Hawke's Bay that I had always thought would be perfect for a restaurant, so obviously we took it. I had often gone there with my grandfather to get fish and chips when I was a child; it was a great location and size, and we could live upstairs.

Within a few months we had packed up Pipi and moved everything to Havelock North. The day we opened was interesting. We got the council consents at about 3 p.m.; the builders and painters finished at about 4; we then filled the room with everything from Greytown and opened at 6. Ants, a friend and cook from Pipi Greytown, came up to help us, so when we did finally open it felt reassuringly like business as usual.

Pipi in Havelock North has evolved. The menu has grown but the philosophy is the same: simple food cooked with attention to detail and care. I am not trying to reinvent the wheel, just perfect and stay true to the original one.

Pipi Havelock is about getting through each night, my family's and other people's; she has had to grow up a bit, as every year has got busier. Just keeping the whole thing intact is a full-time job. But mainly for me, it is about making sure that Mr and Mrs Moggs from Timbuktu on Table 3 are made to feel that they have stumbled upon a part of themselves they like and so leave feeling happy and hopeful.

There are some customers who come to Havelock who used to come to Greytown and even to the coffee business in Wellington before that, which is lovely. And it is equally good when people discover us for the first time.

For me, every day feels like we are starting all over again, every night is different. And I think that, and the support and positive energy we get from the people who come to Pipi, keeps us all going.

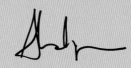

The Land

For me, the land is about memories, moments from my childhood that have stuck with and influenced me for the rest of my life.

Poplar trees always remind me of standing in a big dry paddock with my grandmother, next to a hay barn in Onga Onga. I was going to the bull sales again with my grandparents. Plates of scones and sandwiches, catered by Plunket, were spread out on pressing tables in the woolshed.

The combined smell of causmag, molasses and old leather in a shed at the old Flemington stables on our bottom farm: this is one of the most wonderful smells.

Walking home in the evening from the back paddocks, at that magic time when the light becomes incredibly clear for about half an hour.

It was the beauty of Hawke's Bay that I remembered most when I did not live here and it is largely why I came back. It's not that it was a better childhood than one spent in the city, but just that it was mine and so this is what helps to explain Pipi and give it meaning.

Since leaving the farm, I have always felt like an observer, an outsider. I guess Pipi is my way of creating a place where I belong and feel comfortable.

However, my relationship with the land was for a long time very two-sided; while I loved our farm and felt very at home there, it has taken me a long time to really feel comfortable in this country. There was always a part of me that felt I did not belong or understand what it meant to be a New Zealander. My parents and grandparents very much looked to England;

I went to a very English-style private school. When I was growing up I loved to read books by Vita Sackville-West and Virginia Woolf, the Bloomsbury group. I felt very drawn to their way of life and thinking, and still do. I think this contributed to my feeling of dislocation from New Zealand.

I think this meant I did not have a sense of my place in my country. And while I felt happy in an open paddock, it always worried me that I got an uneasy feeling when I was in the native bush.

It was not until very recently, when I got to know two rather vocal, wild Maori men — one a lawyer for Te Puni Kokiri and the other an artist/builder/activist — that I came to have a true understanding of New Zealand and my place in it. They talked to me about their history here and their beliefs — how tied to the land and to the sea they are. They took me to see an aunty of theirs, who woke me up early and took me to a piece of sacred land not far from where she lived. It might not seem like much, but meeting her and her nephews had a big impact on me. We went to a tangi on her marae, and not once during that time did I feel like I had no right to be there, even though it was all completely foreign to me. Through learning about their connection to everything, the land and the country as a whole, it suddenly came alive. I finally got a real sense of New Zealand even though it was not my history. Somehow feeling New Zealand through them, I have come to understand where I belong, and now I finally feel like a New Zealander.

Rather than sitting on top of the land, I am in it, a part of it.

They also talked to me about their ancestors as very much a part of their lives, and how the native bush is filled with these ancestors' spirits. Then I began to understand why I had always felt uneasy in it; I must have been sensing this. But once I learned this, the discomfort vanished.

Anyway, there it is: we firmly sit in our gumboots in a paddock (eating pizza).

Children

Pipi very much embraces children and their parents; it is their place just as much as anyone else's. In the early evening, the restaurant can be full of families. From the outside I guess it may appear chaotic at times, but as a mother of young children myself, I know what it is like taking children to a restaurant. And I really hope people will always feel quite comfortable bringing their children to Pipi — the odd spilt drink or broken glass or loud squawk is not an issue.

Children help keep everything in perspective; they keep us real. It is a lovely aspect of Pipi that we can celebrate this by making children feel it is one of their places.

friends

The definition of friendship:

Someone with whom you feel completely comfortable, not judged by, who would drop everything and come to your rescue if you needed them to. Someone who unconditionally loves and supports you.

I am not good at keeping in touch, and have lost contact with lots of people over the years. But I still consider them friends and often think about them. Pipi, however, has made lots of friends: customers and people who have worked for her. I do not even know the names of some of them, but they feel like friends and when they come in, whether it is once a year or once a week, it is great to see them.

It is very easy to get so busy that you forget about contacting people, but here we are celebrating the times that you do, as well as the amazing friends who come to Pipi to spend time together.

I love the way Pipi has become a gathering place: local families bring their friends from out of town; older people come and sit for hours, catching up; students, back home for the holidays, often meet for a pizza.

And then there are people who used to come regularly to Pipi who have died. I will not name them, but I would just like to say to their families that we have not forgotten them, and they will always be a part of Pipi's history.

Soup

JERUSALEM ARTICHOKE SOUP

Serves 6
We had lots of Jerusalem artichokes growing wild in our garden when I was a child, and this was a soup my mother often made for lunch. Peeling artichokes before you cook them is rather fiddly; it is much easier to do after boiling, when the skins just fall off. You also catch all the goodness of the skin in the stock.

2kg Jerusalem artichokes
500g potatoes, peeled and
    halved
5 bay leaves
1 dessertspoon oil
1 dessertspoon butter
1 onion, peeled and diced
50g butter
50g flour
250ml milk
salt and white pepper
¼ whole nutmeg, grated
lemon juice to serve
parsley to serve

Wash the artichokes very well and put them in a large saucepan with the potatoes, cover with water and throw in the bay leaves. Bring to the boil and slowly simmer until the vegetables are soft, 20 minutes. Put the artichokes and potatoes somewhere to cool, reserving the liquid. Once the artichokes are cool enough to handle, you can peel them.

Now heat the oil and the dessertspoon of butter in a small frying pan. Add the onion and slowly cook for 10–15 minutes until it is very soft and starting to melt.

In a big saucepan, melt the second measure of butter and then add the flour, stirring continuously on a very low heat for 3 minutes. Meanwhile, heat the milk along with 750ml of the water the vegetables were cooked in until almost boiling, then add this to the flour mix, whisking all the time. Keep stirring on the lowest heat until it boils, then simmer for another 15 minutes, stirring often.

Put the cooked potatoes, artichokes and onion in a blender with the salt and pepper, then whiz until very, very smooth. Add this to the white sauce along with the nutmeg, and there it is — soup.

When serving the soup, squeeze some lemon juice over each bowl and garnish with fresh parsley. Croutons fried with pancetta or bacon, or toasted wholegrain bread are great with this.

SPICY PUMPKIN SOUP

Serves 6

When the small, dark green squash pumpkins are around we use them a lot at Pipi. I know they get used to feed cattle; well, what lucky cattle, I think they are the only pumpkin worth eating. The skins are delicious too, they are great in salads or you can add them to this soup. You just have to wash them well, and not cook them in too much oil.

34 / 35

1 medium-sized dark green squash pumpkin, cut into wedges
2 medium-sized potatoes, peeled and cut into pieces
1 tablespoon olive oil
1 big onion, peeled and thinly sliced
3 tablespoons Green Curry Paste (see page 291)
3–4 litres vegetable stock or water
salt and freshly ground black pepper
1 small bunch fresh coriander, ripped, to garnish

Preheat the oven to 180°C.

Put the pumpkin and potato on an oiled tray and then into the oven. Cook thoroughly until the pumpkin has browned nicely, 35–40 minutes. Take out the vegetables and cool.

Now take a big saucepan, add the oil and then the onion. Stir the onion around in the oil and let it slowly cook until it completely softens. Now add the curry paste and mix it in, letting it cook and brown a little. Then scoop the pumpkin out of its skin and add this to the pan with the potato, reserving the pumpkin skin.

Cover the vegetables with vegetable stock or water and let it all simmer away for 15–20 minutes. Then whiz up the soup in a food processor, with the pumpkin skin if using, in batches until it is very smooth. Season with salt and pepper.

Reheat and serve garnished with coriander and maybe the Savoury Scones on page 182.

WINTERGREEN SOUP

Serves 4–6

We are very lucky in that we have a supplier, Epicurean, who sells wonderful bags of mixed wintergreen: cavolo nero, kale, different silverbeets and spinach. But you can just as easily make up your own mixture from whatever is available. This is also a great opportunity to use things like nettle and beetroot and dandelion leaves, which are all great to eat and very good for you.

100g butter

1 tablespoon oil

4 medium potatoes, peeled and cut into 4

2 leeks, tough leaves discarded, then cut up

5 cloves garlic, peeled

400g mixed wintergreen leaves, tough stems removed

1.2 litres water

1 teaspoon salt

juice of ½ a lemon

½ whole nutmeg, grated

Melt the butter and oil in a saucepan on a low heat, then add the potato, leeks and garlic. Stir until the vegetables are covered with the oily butter and then very slowly cook them for 5 minutes.

Add the leaves to the pan, again stirring well to coat. Now slowly cook for another 15 minutes, stirring every so often so the vegetables do not stick to the bottom of the pan. Then pour in the water and simmer for a further 20 minutes. Now add the salt, lemon juice and nutmeg. Blend it all together in a food processor until very smooth.

Reheat to serve. When you reheat the soup, taste for seasoning and if you feel like it add ½ cup of cream for a richer, smoother flavour — but it is still great without it.

At Pipi we reheat the soup, then roll out a circle of pizza dough and place it over the bowl, putting a knob of garlic butter on top of the dough. We cook and brown the dough in the pizza oven (this would take about 9 minutes in a domestic oven at 250°C).

CARROT, ORANGE AND PEANUT BUTTER SOUP

Serves 6

The idea of peanut butter in a soup may sound a bit odd, but it is not. In fact people loved it when we have had it on the menu at Pipi, and it is great for children.

1 tablespoon olive oil
1 red onion, finely diced
740g carrots, peeled and
    chopped
350g potatoes, peeled and
    chopped
1 orange, skin on, cut into
    8 wedges
6 cloves garlic, peeled
1.5cm knob fresh ginger,
    roughly chopped
200g peanut butter
salt and freshly ground black
    pepper
1 small bunch coriander,
    ripped

Heat the oil gently in a saucepan, then add the onion and stir it around in the oil for a few minutes. Let the onion slowly cook until it is translucent and starting to melt. Now add the carrots, potatoes, orange, garlic and ginger. Mix them all together and let them cook away for about 10 minutes, or until they are wonderfully shiny and starting to brown a little. You will need to stir them quite a lot. Now cover them with water and boil gently until the vegetables are soft, 20–25 minutes.

Take out half of the orange wedges and add the peanut butter. Pour into a food processor and purée the soup, in batches if you need to, until very smooth. Season with salt and pepper.

When you serve the soup, throw the coriander on top. You can add cream, it is up to you.

Risotto

ROAST PUMPKIN AND SPICY SAUSAGE RISOTTO

Serves 4–6
You do not have to add chilli to this, but if you like fiery food then the combination of chilli with pumpkin and sausage is pretty good.

½ large, dark green squash
    pumpkin, cut into medium-
    sized wedges
1 tablespoon olive oil
1 red onion, finely chopped
5 good pork sausages
1½ teaspoons chilli flakes
500g Arborio rice
1 cup white wine
6 sage leaves
1.75 litres chicken stock
25g butter
handful of rocket
½ cup grated Parmesan
salt and freshly ground black
    pepper
1 cup grated Parmesan to
    serve

Preheat the oven to 180°C.

Put the pumpkin in an oiled oven tray and roast for 30–35 minutes until slightly caramelised and soft in the middle.

Place a large, heavy frying pan on a medium heat, add the olive oil then the onion and cook slowly until the onion is completely soft but making sure it does not brown. Take the onion out of the pan and set aside.

Squeeze the sausage meat out of its casings into a bowl and mix in the chilli flakes. Then put small cherry-sized rounds of this mixture into the pan, with more olive oil if you need to, and cook until brown on the outside.

Now put the onion back in the pan and add the rice. Cook, stirring, until the rice is opaque, 2–3 minutes. Add the white wine and sage leaves, and cook gently until the wine evaporates.

Meanwhile, gently heat the chicken stock in another saucepan.

Once the wine has evaporated, start adding the stock 1½ cups at a time, stirring often. As soon as one lot of stock has evaporated, add some more. Do this until the rice is cooked but still has a wee bite to it, 15–20 minutes. You do not want it to be overcooked.

Continued over page

Now remove the skin from the pumpkin and break the pumpkin into bits. Fold this through the rice with the butter, rocket and the grated Parmesan. Season with salt and pepper. Sprinkle more grated Parmesan over each bowl when you serve it.

And there it is.

RED WINE RISOTTO WITH PECORINO AND RADICCHIO

Serves 4

I have also made this risotto with dried porcini mushrooms, which works well. Just soak the mushrooms for 25 minutes and add them towards the end of the cooking time. The red wine you use makes a big difference; traditionally it would be Barolo or Amarone, we use a good Hawke's Bay merlot.

90g butter
1 red onion, finely diced
400g Arborio rice
850ml chicken stock
1 bottle red wine
1 small radicchio
150g pecorino, shaved
salt and freshly ground
    black pepper

Melt 50g of the butter in a big, heavy frying pan, add the onion and cook until very soft. Try not to let it stick to the bottom or brown. Now add the rice and stir it around until it goes opaque — this only takes a few minutes.

Meanwhile, heat the stock to simmering in another saucepan.

Next add three-quarters of the wine to the risotto and keep stirring until it has all been absorbed, then start adding the warm stock a few ladlefuls at a time. Once each lot has been absorbed, add another, stirring often. When all the stock has been absorbed, add the last of the wine, at which point the rice should be cooked. This will take 15–20 minutes.

Turn off the heat and add the rest of the butter. Fold through the radicchio and some of the pecorino, saving most to scatter on the top. Season with salt and pepper.

CHAMPAGNE AND LEEK RISOTTO

Serves 4–6

I love the idea of champagne risotto. It seems rather decadent and also fun, which it is, plus it tastes very good. You do not have to use the very best French champagne but you do taste it, so use a sparkling wine that you would happily drink. It seems such an obvious fit to put salmon with this risotto, but you don't have to. It is lovely with just the leek and the Parmesan, or a little pan-fried prosciutto folded through at the end is good too.

50g butter
1 dessertspoon olive oil
500g leeks, tough outer
    leaves discarded, cut into
    ½cm slices
500g Arborio rice
1 litre bubbly
1 litre chicken stock
50g butter
500g hot smoked salmon
small bunch dill, finely
    chopped (optional)
1 teaspoon salt
white pepper
handful of spinach
½ cup grated Parmesan

Heat the butter and oil in a large, heavy frying pan on medium heat, add the leek and slowly cook until soft, 35–40 minutes.

Then add the rice, stirring until it is opaque, about 3 minutes. Now pour in 250ml of the bubbly and let it cook until all the liquid has been absorbed.

Meanwhile, heat the stock and 500ml of the bubbly in a saucepan and keep it simmering away.

Now add the warm liquid to the rice a cup at a time and keep stirring. When all the liquid has been absorbed, add the last 250ml of bubbly. When this is almost absorbed the risotto should be cooked, 15–20 minutes. You want the rice to have a wee bite with some liquid remaining in the risotto, it shouldn't be the consistency of porridge. Now melt in the second measure of butter and fold through the salmon and the dill if using. Season with salt and pepper.

Fold the spinach through the risotto and serve it with the Parmesan sprinkled on top. Without the salmon, this is also good as a side dish with any baked or pan-fried fish.

Pasta

VODKA, HAM AND BABY PEA PENNE

Serves 2

This is a great quick meal that has lots of flavour and is very comforting. The combination of cream and tomato is always amazing. If you don't feel like meat, roast pumpkin is great instead of ham. Actually, the sauce is very good on its own without ham or pumpkin, maybe just a bit of basil.

knob of butter
4 slices ham, cut into thick strips
1 cup Pipi Tomato Sauce (see page 90) or any good tomato sauce
2 tablespoons vodka
½ cup cream
4 cups cooked pasta
½ cup baby peas
½ cup grated Parmesan
freshly ground black pepper

Heat the butter in a frying pan, add the ham and gently cook for 1 minute. Add the tomato sauce and leave it for a minute to warm through, then add the vodka and then the cream. Cook slowly until the mixture starts to thicken, 5 minutes. Add the pasta and peas, stirring until hot and well mixed into the sauce. Add ¼ cup of Parmesan and a good grind of pepper. Stir these in and then it is ready.

Serve with the remaining Parmesan on top and a salad, some bread and wine.

TO COOK PASTA

Bring a saucepan of water to the boil, add 1 teaspoon of salt and the pasta. Cook until there is just a little resistance when you bite into the pasta, but it is not hard. At Pipi we use penne, but you could use orecchietti or spaghetti — there are no rules. Most of our recipes call for 4 cups of cooked pasta; 2½ cups of dried pasta will give you 4 cups of cooked.

BACON AND BLUE CHEESE PASTA WITH BABY PEAS

Serves 2

This is one of our most popular pasta dishes: people love bacon, don't they? The blue cheese makes it as well. It is rich but that is the point: rich, creamy and uncomplicated.

1½ cups cream
140g good-tasting blue
   cheese
1 tablespoon olive oil
4 rashers bacon
4 cups cooked pasta
½ cup baby peas
½ cup grated Parmesan to
   serve
freshly ground black pepper

Pour the cream into a medium-sized frying pan and crumble the cheese into it. Heat slowly.

Heat the oil in another frying pan and cook the bacon until it is crispy.

When the cream sauce starts to thicken, add the pasta and the peas. Stir them into the sauce until coated and the sauce is thick and shiny, 5 minutes. Now add the crispy bacon.

Pour the pasta into bowls and sprinkle the Parmesan on top. Check the seasoning; you should not need salt because the blue cheese is salty, but ground pepper is important.

FOUR CHEESE PENNE

Serves 2
This is a macaroni cheese for adults who love cheese. You could try it with different combinations of your favourite cheeses.

50g provolone
50g Taleggio
1½ cups cream
½ whole nutmeg, grated
4 cups cooked pasta
2 tablespoons fresh thyme
    leaves
½ cup fresh breadcrumbs
50g fresh mozzarella, ripped
    into pieces
½ cup Parmesan
freshly ground black pepper

Preheat the oven grill to 200°C.

Crumble the provolone and Taleggio into an ovenproof frying pan, add the cream and slowly melt it all together over a medium heat. Next add the nutmeg and the cooked pasta and stir this until it is thoroughly coated with the sauce.

Mix the thyme leaves with the breadcrumbs.

Take the pasta off the heat and place the ripped mozzarella on top. Sprinkle the breadcrumbs and thyme over this and then the grated Parmesan. Season with pepper. Place under the grill until the breadcrumbs become crispy and the cheese melts and starts to brown, 5 minutes.

Serve at once with a big salad; iceberg, parsley and rocket would be good.

You could also fold through some spinach when you add the pasta.

CABBAGE, BACON AND MASCARPONE PENNE

Serves 2

Cabbage is one of those vegetables that is rather forgotten about. It is very good pan-fried with a little butter and bacon — hopefully this pasta dish will get you inspired to use it more.

2 cups savoy cabbage, cut into fine strips
2 cups red cabbage, cut into fine strips
1 tablespoon olive oil
4 rashers bacon, cut into pieces
¼ cup cream
½ cup mascarpone
4 cups cooked pasta
1 tablespoon finely ripped dill
salt and freshly ground black pepper
½ cup grated Parmesan to serve

Put the savoy and red cabbage into a colander and pour boiling water over.

Heat the oil in a frying pan and cook the bacon until crisp. Add the cabbage and cook slowly, stirring often, until it is just soft.

Add the cream and the mascarpone, and mix them in well. Let it all cook together for about 5 minutes until the sauce thickens. Fold through the cooked pasta and the dill, and season with salt and pepper.

Serve with the grated Parmesan sprinkled over.

ANCHOVY AND CAVOLO NERO PENNE

Serves 2

I find that people who like anchovies don't want them mucked around with, so we make this pasta very strong so there is no chance of them wondering where the anchovies are. The anchovy paste will keep for several days in the fridge; it is also good spread on toast or a pizza.

½ cup anchovies
8 cloves garlic
¼ cup parsley
½ cup extra virgin olive oil
1 tablespoon pinenuts
8 medium-sized leaves
  cavolo nero, stalks
  removed
4 cups cooked pasta
juice of ½ a lemon
grated Parmesan to serve
freshly ground black pepper

Dice up the anchovies with the garlic and parsley until almost a paste. You can do this in the food processor, but there is something nice about doing it by hand and I think the texture is better. Add the extra virgin olive oil.

Put a dash of olive oil in a frying pan and gently heat. Add the anchovy paste and stir for a couple of minutes. Now add the pinenuts, letting them gently brown, stirring all the time. Next put in the cavolo nero and let it wilt. Then add the pasta and keep stirring until it is well mixed through and the pasta is coated with the anchovy paste and the cavolo nero has softened. If you need to add more olive oil, then do so. If some of the pasta starts to brown slightly, don't worry — it tastes good.

Stir through the lemon juice and serve with grated Parmesan and lots of pepper.

SAUSAGE AND MUSTARD PENNE

Serves 2

2 pork sausages
½ tablespoon fennel seeds
1 tablespoon olive oil
½ cup white wine
½ cup cream
4 dessertspoons seeded
   mustard
4 cups cooked pasta
1 cup grated Parmesan
salt and freshly ground black
   pepper
small bunch basil, ripped

Squeeze the sausage meat out of the casings into a bowl and mix in the fennel seeds. Shape the meat into little balls the size of sparrow's eggs or maybe a bit smaller.

Heat the olive oil in a big frying pan and cook the meatballs all the way through, until crisp on the outside. Add the wine and cook until it reduces by about a third. Now add the cream and the mustard. Cook until the sauce starts to thicken, 5–7 minutes. Add the cooked pasta and keep simmering until the sauce is quite thick and coats the pasta.

Next stir in half of the grated Parmesan and season with salt and pepper.

Serve with the remaining grated Parmesan and basil. I often sprinkle over flat-leaf parsley, but maybe that is because I love parsley. French tarragon would also be good.

PIPI MEATBALLS WITH PENNE

Serves 4–6 (makes 20 meatballs)
You do not have to put these meatballs with a sauce. They are good on their own for a picnic or in school lunches.

For the meatballs

1kg good beef mince
zest of 1½ lemons
¾ cup grated Parmesan
½ cup finely chopped parsley
1 egg, beaten
2 slices good white bread, soaked in milk and broken into little pieces
½ teaspoon salt and freshly ground black pepper

500g cooked penne
6 cups Pipi Tomato Sauce (see page 90) or any good tomato sauce
1 cup Kalamata olives
150g grated Parmesan to serve

Preheat the oven to 180°C.

For the meatballs, mix everything together in a big bowl with your hands until blended properly. Then shape the mixture into meatballs of around 65g, about the size of a lime. These don't have to be perfectly shaped; if they are slightly rough then those bits will get that nice crunch when you brown them.

Place the meatballs in an oiled oven tray and cook in the oven for 20 minutes or until they are just cooked through. You will need to pull one apart to check they are done.

Now take a large ovenproof dish and put in the cooked meatballs and pasta, the tomato sauce and olives. Mix together then put in the oven and cook for 20–25 minutes until the sauce has been warmed through and reduced slightly.

Serve in bowls, sprinkled with grated Parmesan.

DUCK PAPPARDELLE

Serves 4

There is something about pappardelle that everyone seems to love — when it is served with a slowly braised meat sauce it is fantastic. Duck is now widely available — you don't have to wait until May and get up at dawn to get hold of some.

2 tablespoons olive oil
1 large whole duck
1 red onion, peeled and cut into small pieces
2 medium-sized red kumara, peeled and cut into 1cm pieces
60g pancetta, diced into 1cm pieces
1 orange, cut into quarters
2 whole bulbs garlic, unpeeled
good-sized knob fresh ginger
5 bay leaves
5 sage leaves
750ml white wine
450ml chicken stock
1 teaspoon salt
100ml sweet marsala
freshly ground black pepper
8 cups cooked pappardelle
small bunch flat-leaf parsley, ripped

Preheat the oven to 160°C.

Heat the olive oil in a high-sided casserole which can go on the hob and in the oven, and in which the duck will fit snugly. Put the duck in the dish and brown all over, then remove and set aside.

Now put the onion, kumara, pancetta and orange into the dish and gently brown until they start to caramelise. It is very important that you take your time over this, stirring often and letting the vegetables slowly soften and cook until the kumara is a lovely golden brown.

Put the duck back into the dish, breast side down, along with the garlic bulbs, ginger and the bay and sage leaves. Pour in the wine, return to the hob and let it evaporate by a third. Now add the stock — the duck should be almost covered with liquid, so if it isn't, add more stock. Tightly cover the dish with tin foil and a lid.

Put in the oven and cook for 2 hours. If a lot of liquid evaporates during the cooking, add more, but if you seal the dish well you should not need to. When the meat is falling off the bones, the duck is cooked.

Take the duck out of the liquid, reserving the liquid, and when cool enough to handle, pull all the meat from the bones. Discard the orange and sage and bay leaves.

Continued over page

Cool the cooking liquid until the fat settles on the top and you can easily scrape it off. Then squeeze the garlic out of the bulbs back into the liquid and throw away the skins. Add the salt and marsala to the liquid and put it back on a medium heat until it has reduced a little. Then put the duck meat and the cooked pappardelle into the sauce and stir it all together until everything is coated. Check the seasoning.

Pile onto a big platter and cover with flat-leaf parsley. Eat with good sourdough bread and an iceberg lettuce salad dressed with a hazelnut dressing.

For a hazelnut dressing, put the following ingredients into a blender: 8 tablespoons hazelnut oil, 2 tablespoons champagne vinegar, 2 teaspoons Dijon mustard, 4 tablespoons dry toasted hazelnuts, and salt and pepper to taste. Whiz until all the ingredients are blended and the nuts are roughly chopped but not too fine.

PUTTANESCA

Serves 4

Traditionally spaghetti is used to make Puttanesca; we use penne, but it is up to you. I tend to put a little more sauce with the pasta than some might, but I think that it has such a delicious flavour, you want to really taste it. This is a useful sauce. Great on a pizza — just spread it onto a base and top with fresh mozzarella. Or follow the recipe below but fold the sauce through potato gnocchi (see page 78) instead of the pasta. I prefer buying olives with pits and then pitting them as they have a better flavour.

7 cloves garlic, roughly chopped
10 anchovies, roughly chopped
2 tablespoons olive oil
250g black olives, pits removed, roughly chopped
2½ tablespoons capers, roughly chopped
2 x 400g cans whole peeled Italian tomatoes, drained and mashed
1 tablespoon sugar
1½ teaspoons chilli flakes
8 cups cooked pasta
large bunch of basil, if in season
1 cup grated Parmesan

In a large frying pan, cook the garlic and anchovies in the olive oil until the garlic is golden and the anchovies start to melt. Now add the olives, capers, tomatoes, sugar and chilli and let it all simmer gently for about 20 minutes until the sauce has reduced and the flavours have developed.

Now add the cooked pasta to the sauce and mix it all together until the pasta is completely coated, adding more olive oil if you need to.

Fold through the basil, if using, and serve in bowls with the Parmesan grated over the top.

BASIL PESTO PASTA

Serves 2

I love the idea of a big bowl of basil pesto pasta, simple and unadulterated except for some beautiful wee new potatoes. I think it is a minor scandal the way pesto gets mixed with anything and everything. I do think it has detracted from the glory of its traditional use, but there you go, that is just me. Beans are sometimes added as well, which can be cooked in the same water as the pasta — perfect. When basil is in season it really is worth making pesto yourself, then folding it through some pasta and just sitting quietly and enjoying it.

8 small new potatoes, skins on, washed

4 cups cooked pasta

1 cup Basil Pesto (see page 288)

handful of fresh basil

½ cup grated Parmesan

Steam the potatoes over simmering water until just soft. Combine with the pasta.

While the potatoes and pasta are still warm, fold through the pesto. Spoon into bowls and top with the fresh basil and grated Parmesan.

LEEK, MUSHROOM AND GOAT'S CHEESE LASAGNE

Serves 4

OK, so this is not something you will whip up in 10 minutes after work, but actually it is not that complicated. You could cook the leeks the day before and if you used fresh lasagne sheets, you would not have to pre-cook them. So grab a glass of wine or scotch or a cup of tea, put on Bonnie Prince Billy's album *Ease Down the Road* and go to it. Also this is the perfect meal to make as a gift; you must care deeply about the person to have laboured long and hard to make this thing of beauty.

150g butter

6 leeks, tough leaves discarded, washed and cut into 2cm thick rings

1 tablespoon olive oil

50g flour

1 litre milk

8 sheets lasagne

1kg field mushrooms, wiped and cut into ½cm slices

6 sprigs thyme

250g goat's cheese

¼ cup grated Parmesan

Preheat the oven to 180°C.

Melt 75g of the butter in a saucepan on a gentle heat and add the leeks along with the olive oil. You want to cook these as slowly as you can until they are very soft, which will take about 45 minutes. Stir them often so they do not catch on the bottom of the pan or brown.

For the béchamel sauce, melt 50g of the butter in another saucepan, then take off the heat and add the flour. Put back on the heat and, stirring all the time, cook for 4 minutes. Now add the milk, stirring until it is all mixed together. Then gently cook, stirring often, for 15 minutes. The béchamel will have thickened in this time. Take off the heat and cover with greaseproof paper until you are ready to use it.

Bring a large saucepan of salted water to the boil and add the lasagne sheets, cooking them until they are just soft.

Melt the remaining 25g of the butter in a large skillet, then slowly cook the mushrooms with the thyme until they have released all their juices and are soft. This will not take long, about 6 minutes. Take the mushrooms out of the skillet and drain on a paper towel so some of the moisture

Continued over page

is absorbed. Discard the thyme sprigs. Now everything is cooked and you are ready to assemble the lasagne.

At Pipi we make our lasagne in loaf tins as they are nice and high and the perfect shape, but any ovenproof dish that will hold a lasagne for 4 people will do.

First, put a thin layer of béchamel sauce on the bottom of the dish, then a sheet of lasagne. Put half the leeks on top of this and then another thin layer of sauce, then another sheet of lasagne. Now add more sauce, topped with half of the mushrooms and followed by half of the goat's cheese sprinkled on top. Next another layer of lasagne, then sauce, then the other half of the leeks. Next is another layer of sauce, then lasagne, the remaining mushrooms and the rest of the goats' cheese sprinkled on top. Finish with the grated Parmesan.

Cook in the oven for about 40 minutes, until the sauce starts bubbling up to the top.

You do not need much with the lasagne, just a green salad — radicchio and rocket would be perfect — and a glass of wine.

POTATO GNOCCHI

Serves 6
Gnocchi is one of those recipes that can be a bit intimidating, but it really is worth making. It is not difficult and is very satisfying to make and eat.

1kg potatoes, Agria are good, peeled
200g flour
⅓ teaspoon salt
1 egg, beaten

Line a baking tray with greaseproof paper.

Cook the potatoes in boiling salted water until soft. Drain them really well and leave them in a colander for 10 minutes to completely dry out. Now mash the potato, or better still put though a ricer while still warm — you want to get out all the lumps, so do whatever it takes.

When the mashed potato is cool, put it on the bench and sift over the flour and salt. Mix together with your hands. Now make a hollow in the middle and pour in the beaten egg. Mix it all in with your hands. The thing with gnocchi is that you don't want to over-handle it. So you need a light hand and as soon as everything is blended together, stop.

Bring a big saucepan of water to the boil.

Now divide the mixture in two, and roll each piece into a long sausage shape, 2cm high and 6cm wide.

Flour a knife and cut the gnocchi sausages into 2cm pieces. At this point most people shape them with a fork. I don't because I feel this desire to make them beautiful results in tough gnocchi. When trying to shape them, they are over-handled and become hard. Anyway it is up to you, but after cutting them I put them straight onto a baking tray.

Once the water is boiling, drop in the gnocchi. Don't do too many at a time because once they rise to the surface you want to be able to remove them straight away, using a

Continued over page

slotted spoon. This is important; if they stay in the water they will become waterlogged.

Now you can fold them through a sauce and eat them, or you can put them back on the tray to cool. At this point, they will keep on the bench for a few hours, or in the fridge overnight. You can also freeze gnocchi: place the tray in the freezer and once frozen put them in bags.

NETTLE GNOCCHI

Nettle is very good for you; among other things, it is high in iron. Normally found growing around woolsheds and under trees in spring and summer, this plant is not as scary as it might first seem — as long as you handle it with care, you will not get stung. Wear gloves when you pick it and plunge it into a saucepan of boiling water to take the sting out of it.

Nettle can be used in place of spinach, and is great in green soups, but works really well with gnocchi.

Nettle gnocchi goes well with either the ragu or the sage butter sauces (see pages 286), or even as a side dish with salmon or lamb chops.

Cook a shopping bag full of nettle until it is just soft, about 5 minutes. Then drain and remove and discard the thick stalks. Cut up the nettle really finely. This should give you about 250g of cooked nettle.

Now it can be added to the gnocchi at the same time as the flour and egg. Then just follow the same method.

PORCINI GNOCCHI

Soak 25g dried porcini mushrooms in hot water for 20 minutes and then drain well. Cut the mushrooms into small pieces and add to the potato at the same time as the flour and egg. Then just follow the same method.

POTATO GNOCCHI WITH TOMATO RAGU

Serves 2

At Pipi we freeze our gnocchi and then use them as we need them. This recipe will work just as well with fresh gnocchi, they will just be a little bit more delicate.

1 tablespoon olive oil

16 Potato Gnocchi, fresh or frozen (see page 78)

¼ cup flour

2 cups Pipi Tomato Sauce (see page 90) or any good tomato sauce

8 leaves spinach

½ cup grated Parmesan

Preheat the oven to 250°C.

Heat the olive oil in an ovenproof frying pan. Dust the frozen gnocchi very lightly with the flour and drop them into the pan. Brown these gently on one side then turn them over and put the pan in the oven.

Cook in the oven, checking after about 5 minutes. They should be lightly brown all over and slightly puffed up. They will probably need another 5 minutes.

Remove from the oven and strain the oil from the pan. Then add the tomato sauce around and over the gnocchi. Put back into the oven for another 10 minutes or until the sauce has reduced a little and is hot and glossy.

Fold the spinach through and spoon into bowls. Top with the grated Parmesan.

PORCINI GNOCCHI WITH SAGE BUTTER

Serves 2
Sage butter is rich but you are not going to have it every day, are you?

1 tablespoon olive oil
16 Porcini Gnocchi, fresh or
    frozen (see page 80)
¼ cup flour
100g butter
12 sage leaves
½ cup grated Parmesan

Heat the olive oil in an ovenproof frying pan. Dust the frozen gnocchi very lightly with the flour and drop them into the pan. Brown them gently on one side then turn them over and put the pan in the oven.

Cook, checking after about 5 minutes. They should be lightly brown all over and slightly puffed up. They will probably need another 5 minutes.

Remove from the oven and strain the oil from the pan.

Meanwhile, melt the butter in a pan, add the sage leaves and slowly cook until the butter turns a beautiful nutty brown and starts to foam, and the sage is crisp. Then take the pan off the hob straight away as you do not want to burn the butter.

Put the gnocchi on a warmed plate, pour the sage butter over, then top with the grated Parmesan.

Pizza

People often think we are an Italian restaurant, but we are not. We do pizza because it is quite simply a great thing to eat. The inspiration for the Pipi pizza came from one I had while in Florence with my uncle. He was an artist and during the day we walked for miles looking at paintings of madonnas and at churches and sculptures, and he would talk to me about why they were important. It was great but what I really enjoyed was when we would go out for dinner at night to one of the restaurants near where we were staying. It was years ago, but a meal I had at one of these restaurants has defined pizza for me ever since: very thin base, not much topping, strong flavours, simple. The thingI remember best was a lovely warm night walking around Florence, the beauty of the city and its history, mostly the deep, deep blue of the chapel ceilings.

Here are the recipes for our pizza dough and the tomato sauce we use on our pizzas, as well as a few of our toppings, some of which we make all the time and some we make when the ingredients are in season.

PIZZA DOUGH

Over the years we have experimented with different dough recipes, but this is the one that has stuck. It has great flavour and allows you to roll it out very thinly. At Pipi we hand-roll all our pizzas to order and I think this is necessary to get the best result.

For 4 medium-sized pizzas

500g flour
3 teaspoons caster sugar
1 teaspoon salt
280ml lukewarm water
35ml olive oil
10g fresh yeast or 1 teaspoon dried yeast

For 8 medium-sized pizzas

1kg flour
6 teaspoons caster sugar
2 teaspoons salt
550ml lukewarm water
70ml olive oil
20g fresh yeast or 2 teaspoons dried yeast

Mix the flour, sugar and salt together in a bowl. Mix the warm water, oil and yeast together in a jug. Put the dry ingredients in the bowl of an electric mixer with a dough hook, then pour the wet ingredients on top. Turn the mixer on and let it knead away for 3 minutes, then take the dough out. If you don't have a dough hook or would prefer to make the dough by hand, bring the dry and wet ingredients together in a bowl, then turn the dough out onto a lightly floured bench and knead for 10 minutes. There is nothing better for the soul than kneading bread. Then put the dough in an oiled bowl and cover.

Now put the dough in a warm place and let it double in size. This will take about an hour, but it depends a lot on the time of year and how warm it is. Once doubled in size, knock the dough back and divide into four or eight balls depending on the quantity you have made. Let these rise for about 10 minutes so they will be easier to roll.

When ready to roll out the dough, lightly flour the bench — if you use too much flour it will affect the dough while it cooks, so use just enough to stop the dough from sticking. I think pizzas should be rather rustic in shape, so you do not want perfect rounds. To achieve this, try to roll the dough into a square shape, turning it over every so often. It must also be evenly rolled or some of the edges will cook faster than others. You want the finished base to be just a little larger than the pizza tray, so a few bits should hang over.

TOPPING A PIZZA

I think topping a pizza is like making a sandwich, in that when you are making one, you need to consider what each bite will taste like. You need to arrange the ingredients so that each mouthful will get a little bit of everything or enough of something to make it delicious. But you do not want it to look like you have got out the ruler; your pizza must look like it was hand-made, not at all symmetrical or organised. If you use just a few very tasty ingredients that complement each other, then they will turn an ordinary pizza into something indescribable.

PIZZA CHEESE

At Pipi, the basic cheese that we sprinkle on the pizzas is grated 'pizza cheese'. You can buy this at the supermarket already made up or blend it yourself: half mozzarella (fresh if you like), a quarter cheddar and a quarter Parmesan.

COOKING PIZZA

A commercial pizza oven is set to about 400°C, so when cooking them at home you want to have your oven as hot as possible, 250°C, and on fan bake, which will help to cook the top at the same time as the bottom. The cooking time will depend on how much topping you have put on them. One of our cooks, Kelly, often makes pizzas at home with her children, and the ones they load up with tomato and cheese take a lot longer to cook. But what a great way to get your children cooking!

A pizza will normally take about 10 minutes to cook and should be able to be rolled up and eaten in your hands. So to achieve this, you do not want to overcook it. What you are aiming for is the toppings to be well cooked and the cheese really melted. The base should be just light brown and the edges the same. It will not cook absolutely evenly, but that is the charm of pizzas.

The recipes are all for a medium-sized pizza tray, which is around 30cm in diameter. We use pizza trays, but baking trays work just as well. It's nice to sprinkle polenta over the tray before placing the pizzas on them. This adds flavour and texture while also preventing the pizza from sticking.

PIPI TOMATO SAUCE

Makes 1.5 litres (6 cups)
This is our basic sauce which we use on all our pizzas and in some of the
pasta dishes. The sauce is also great to have with sausages. It is important
to use whole rather than crushed tomatoes.

25ml olive oil
10g garlic, finely chopped
4 x 400g cans whole peeled
    Italian tomatoes
75g soft brown sugar
200g tomato paste
2 teaspoons salt
½ teaspoon freshly ground
    black pepper

Place the olive oil in a saucepan on a low heat, add the
chopped garlic and cook slowly until it just starts to
become golden and gives off a wonderful smell. Now add
everything else and let the sauce cook away on a gentle
heat for about 1–1½ hours. You will need to keep a close
eye on it, stirring often so it does not stick. When the
sauce is ready it will have reduced a bit and gone a lovely
deep red.

When the sauce has cooled a little, give it a good mash to
get out any big lumps of tomato, then pour the sauce into
a container. You can mash the tomatoes before you cook
them as well. It will keep for 1 week in the fridge.

PIPI PIZZA BREAD

Makes 1 pizza bread

1 dessertspoon polenta,
  optional
200g Pizza Dough (see page
  88)
2 tablespoons olive oil

Preheat the oven to 250°C.

Oil a baking tray and shake on the polenta if you're using it. Now roll out the dough and brush with the olive oil.

Assemble with one of the toppings over the page.

Put in the oven and bake for 5–8 minutes. Pizza breads are cooked when they have pale brown speckles on the top or bottom of the bases.

GARLIC CONFIT
PIZZA BREAD

GARLIC PIZZA BREAD

25g Garlic Butter (see page 286)
1 Pizza Bread base
1 teaspoon rosemary leaves

Break up the garlic butter and scatter on top of the prepared base. Then sprinkle with the rosemary.

Cook for 5–8 minutes in the oven.

POTATO, TRUFFLE OIL AND ROSEMARY PIZZA BREAD

25g Pizza Cheese (see page 89)
1 Pizza Bread base
2 medium-sized waxy potatoes, peeled and steamed or boiled, grated
drizzle truffle oil
drizzle light olive oil
salt and freshly ground black pepper
1 teaspoon rosemary leaves

Sprinkle a thin layer of the pizza cheese over the prepared base. Cover this with a good layer of the grated cooked potato, then drizzle a small amount of truffle oil over the whole pizza. Finally shake over some light olive oil, season with salt and pepper and sprinkle over the rosemary leaves.

Cook for 5–8 minutes in the oven.

GARLIC CONFIT PIZZA BREAD

1½ bulbs Garlic Confit (see page 294)
1 Pizza Bread base
30g fresh mozzarella, ripped into pieces
1 tablespoon fresh oregano leaves
salt and freshly ground pepper

Squeeze the garlic out of its skin onto the prepared base, making sure it is evenly spaced and letting lots of the garlicky oil spill out. Scatter the mozzarella along with the oregano over the garlic. A little salt and pepper, and then into the oven.

Cook for 5–8 minutes in the oven.

POTATO,
TRUFFLE OIL
AND ROSEMARY
PIZZA BREAD

ASPARAGUS, MINT AND LEMON PIZZA

Makes 1 medium-sized pizza
It is very exciting each year when asparagus comes into season and we can make this pizza. It is also the first sign that summer is almost here.

1 dessertspoon polenta (optional)
200g Pizza Dough (see page 88)
2 tablespoons olive oil
25g Pizza Cheese (see page 89)
10 asparagus spears, approximately
1 lemon, finely sliced
3 tablespoons ripped fresh mint
30g fresh mozzarella, ripped into pieces
15g grated Parmesan
salt and pepper

Preheat the oven to 250°C.

Oil a baking tray and shake on the polenta if you're using it. Now roll out the dough and brush with the olive oil. Sprinkle over a very thin layer of the pizza cheese.

Blanch the asparagus spears in boiling water until just cooked, 2–3 minutes.

Lay the asparagus randomly on the base and then scatter the lemon, mint and fresh mozzarella pieces over the top. Next sprinkle with the grated Parmesan, splash over some olive oil and season with salt and pepper.

Cook for 10–15 minutes in the oven.

CALAMARI PIZZA

Makes 1 medium-sized pizza

1 dessertspoon polenta
   (optional)
200g Pizza Dough (see page
   88)
2 tablespoons olive oil
1½ squid tubes, cut into
   ¼cm wide rings
½ a lemon, very thinly sliced
15g Garlic Butter (see page
   286)
2 tablespoons ripped dill
salt and freshly ground black
   pepper

Preheat the oven to 250°C.

Oil a baking tray and shake on the polenta if you're using it. Now roll out the dough and brush with the olive oil. Place the calamari evenly over the base and then dot the lemon and the garlic butter around the calamari. Sprinkle over the dill and season with salt and pepper. Finally shake some olive oil over the whole thing.

Cook for 10–15 minutes in the oven.

ANCHOVY, POTATO, TALEGGIO AND THYME PIZZA

Makes 1 medium-sized pizza

1 dessertspoon polenta (optional)
200g Pizza Dough (see page 88)
2 tablespoons olive oil
25g Pizza Cheese (see page 89)
1½ medium-sized potatoes, waxy variety best, steamed or boiled with skin on, and cut into ½cm slices
9 anchovies
40g Taleggio, sliced
2 teaspoons thyme leaves
salt and freshly ground black pepper

Preheat the oven to 250°C.

Oil a baking tray and shake on the polenta if you're using it. Now roll out the dough and brush with the olive oil. Sprinkle the base with the pizza cheese, lay the potato slices over the top and then place the anchovies, Taleggio, and thyme on top of the potatoes. Season with salt and pepper, then sprinkle over some olive oil.

Cook for 10–15 minutes in the oven.

PROSCIUTTO AND RICOTTA PIZZA

Makes 1 medium-sized pizza

1 dessertspoon polenta
  (optional)
200g Pizza Dough (see page
  88)
4 tablespoons Pipi Tomato
  Sauce (see page 90)
25g Pizza Cheese (see page
  89)
3 slices prosciutto
30g ricotta
25g Parmesan
salt and freshly ground black
  pepper
small handful of basil leaves,
  ripped

Preheat the oven to 250°C.

Oil a baking tray and shake on the polenta if you're using it. Now roll out the dough and spoon the tomato sauce over it, then sprinkle on the pizza cheese. Spread the prosciutto evenly over the base and then place spoonfuls of ricotta around and on top of it. Sprinkle over the Parmesan and season with salt and pepper.

Cook for 10-15 minutes in the oven. When the pizza is cooked, scatter the basil over the top.

MARGHERITA PIZZA

Makes 1 medium-sized pizza

1 dessertspoon polenta,
   optional
200g Pizza Dough (see page
   88)
4 tablespoons Pipi Tomato
   Sauce (see page 90)
25g Pizza Cheese (see page
   89)
10 cherry tomatoes
30g fresh mozzarella, ripped
   into pieces
salt and freshly ground black
   pepper
1 tablespoon extra virgin
   olive oil
1 teaspoon chilli flakes
   (optional)
small handful of basil leaves,
   ripped

Preheat the oven to 250°C.

Oil a baking tray and shake on the polenta if you're using
it. Now roll out the dough and spread the tomato sauce
over it, then sprinkle the pizza cheese evenly on top.
Place the cherry tomatoes and the mozzarella on the
base and then season with salt and pepper and a good lug
of extra virgin olive oil. If you like chilli, then sprinkle
some on now.

Cook for 10–15 minutes in the oven. When the pizza is
cooked, scatter the basil leaves on top.

BLOKE'S BREAKFAST PIZZA

Makes 1 medium-sized pizza
We started making this at Pipi in Greytown when we were open for breakfast,
but people soon began asking for it late into the night.

1 dessertspoon polenta,
   optional
200g Pizza Dough (see page
   88)
4 tablespoons Pipi Tomato
   Sauce (see page 90)
25g Pizza Cheese (see page
   89)
4 button mushrooms, finely
   sliced
1 medium-sized potato,
   skin on, waxy variety best,
   steamed or boiled, and cut
   into ½cm slices
1 egg
1 small sausage, meat
   squeezed out of the casing
   and rolled into small balls
2 rashers bacon
salt and freshly ground black
   pepper

Preheat the oven to 250°C.

Oil a baking tray and shake on the polenta if you're using
it. Now roll out the dough and spread the tomato sauce
over it and sprinkle the pizza cheese on top of that. Scatter
the mushrooms over the base and then the potato. Now
break the egg on top and place the sausage balls and the
bacon around it. Season with salt and pepper.

Cook for 10–15 minutes in the oven and there it is.

BIG 'SQUARE' PIZZA

Serves 6

Big square pizzas are often sold by the slice. In Venice, I remember buying a slice cut from a large rectangular pizza with a slightly thicker base than normal. These are a great thing to make when you have to feed a lot of people, or if you're going on a picnic.

2 dessertspoons polenta (optional)
600g Pizza Dough (see page 88)
8 tablespoons Pipi Tomato Sauce (see page 90)
60g Pizza Cheese (see page 89)
15 slices pepperoni
handful of capers
10 Kalamata olives
60g fresh mozzarella, ripped into pieces
small handful of basil leaves
salt and freshly ground black pepper

Preheat the oven to 250°C.

Oil a 30cm x 40cm baking tray and shake on the polenta if you're using it. Now roll out the dough and spread the tomato sauce over the base, then sprinkle the pizza cheese on top. Next, evenly place the pepperoni, capers and olives over the base. Now add the mozzarella and sprinkle with the basil leaves, and season with salt and pepper.

It will take a little longer to cook than a normal pizza, 15–20 minutes. Just keep checking it after 10 minutes.

Meat

VEAL MARSALA

Serves 2
This dish has become a staple on our menu. We use a sweet marsala, which I think makes the sauce, but you could use a dry one if you prefer. Tenderloin is the best cut of meat to use for this recipe — two pieces per person is good.

4 veal tenderloins
¼ cup flour
generous knob of butter
dash of olive oil
1 cup sweet marsala
1 cup cream
salt and freshly ground black
    pepper

First put the veal in between two pieces of greaseproof paper and hit it with a meat tenderiser or a rolling pin until it is very thin, about 3mm. Dust the veal very lightly with the flour.

On a medium heat, put the butter and oil in a frying pan large enough to easily hold two pieces of veal. When the butter is sizzling, add two tenderloins, brown them very quickly on both sides and then take them out. Keep warm while you cook the next two. Once they are cooked, remove and keep warm.

Pour off any excess butter, then pour in the marsala and let it reduce a little. Next add the cream. Cook these together slowly for 2–3 minutes until a lovely thick sauce forms. Now put all of the meat back in and swirl the pan so the meat gets a good coating of sauce. Taste and season with salt and pepper if you need to.

Serve the meat on warmed plates and pour the sauce over the top.

At Pipi we serve this with roast potatoes and spinach cooked with lemon. It is also good with buttery fettuccine, or mashed potatoes and broccoli.

VEAL WITH MUSHROOMS AND BRANDY

Serves 2
This is a variation on the previous recipe, equally delicious!

4 veal tenderloins
¼ cup flour
2 knobs of butter
dash of olive oil
2 cups finely diced button
  mushroom
small bunch of fresh thyme,
  leaves only
1 cup brandy
1 cup cream
salt and freshly ground black
  pepper

First put the veal in between two pieces of greaseproof paper and hit it with a meat tenderiser or a rolling pin until it is very thin, about 3mm. Dust the veal very lightly with the flour.

On a medium heat, put 1 knob of butter and the oil in a pan large enough to easily hold two pieces of veal. When the butter is sizzling, add two tenderloins, brown them very quickly on both sides and then take them out. Keep these warm while you cook the next two. Once they are cooked, remove and keep warm.

Now add the other knob of butter to the pan and when it has melted, add the button mushrooms and the thyme and stir until the mushrooms start to brown a little. Next add the brandy, letting it reduce a little. Then pour in the cream and cook for 2–3 minutes until the sauce starts to thicken. Check for seasoning, adding salt and pepper. Put all of the veal back in the pan just long enough for it to warm through and become coated with the sauce.

Serve the meat on warmed plates and pour the sauce over it. You want to eat this with mashed roast celeriac or Brussels sprouts, and perhaps a glass of syrah.

BRAISED LAMB SHOULDER AND KUMARA PIE

Serves 6–8

We have tried lots of different types of meat for our pie but I think lamb has to be the most popular. Different cuts of lamb can be used; we use shoulder, shanks or neck chop. The shoulders are probably the best — I think the meat has more flavour than the other cuts, but they are all good. The wine needs to be one you would happily drink, not a bottle that has been sitting around for a while and has turned into vinegar. I think anything with tomatoes in it is helped with a little sugar, and a lot of reducing, but rather than just adding sugar it is better to use a fruit jelly that has flavour as well as sweetness.

¼ cup flour

3kg lamb shoulder

2 large onions, peeled and sliced

2 big red kumara, peeled and cut into big chunks

2 whole bulbs garlic, tops almost cut off

2 big stalks rosemary

1 teaspoon chilli flakes

¾ bottle white wine

4 x 400g cans whole peeled Italian tomatoes

2 dessertspoons fruit jelly, redcurrant or quince

salt and freshly ground black pepper

2 good handfuls of spinach

500g Pizza Dough (see page 88)

150g Garlic Butter (see page 286)

Preheat the oven to 160°C.

Lightly shake the flour over the lamb. Place a large roasting dish across two hobs on a medium heat and add a good lug of olive oil. Once the oil has heated, brown the lamb all over and then take it out.

Now put the onion and kumara in the dish, adding more oil if you need to. Cook the vegetables slowly and lovingly on a moderate heat until they have softened and browned a little.

Then add the garlic, rosemary, chilli flakes and browned lamb to the pan with the vegetables. Next add the wine and reduce it by a third. Squash up the tomatoes a bit and add them to the pan. The meat needs to be pretty much covered with liquid, so if it is not, add more tomatoes and wine. Cover with tin foil, sealing the dish well.

Now place the dish in the oven and cook slowly until the meat is falling off the bones. This can take 5 hours, depending on your oven and the size of the lamb.

Continued over page

Once the lamb is cooked, take the whole shoulder, garlic and kumara out of the dish and set aside to cool. Put the dish with the remaining sauce in the fridge for half an hour, until the fat settles on the top and can be easily skimmed off.

When the meat is cool enough to handle, pull it apart, getting rid of all the fat and bone. You should have lovely pieces of tender lamb.

Now put the roasting dish with the sauce back on the hob on a medium heat. Add the jelly, squeeze the garlic cloves out their skins into the sauce and season with salt and pepper. Reduce gently to intensify the flavours until you are happy with the taste. Now put the meat and the kumara back into the sauce and mix it all through. There it is, the filling for a great pie.

Preheat the oven to 250°C.

At Pipi, what we would do now is put servings of this into individual ovenproof bowl with some spinach, and cover them with a round of our pizza dough, cut to fit and spread with garlic butter. You could, however, make it into one big pie and use puff pastry instead of pizza dough.

Then put the pie in a very hot oven and cook for 5–8 minutes or until the dough is light brown and cooked through.

You could also stir the lamb and kumara filling through pasta such as pappardelle or serve with mashed potatoes or toasted Parmesan polenta.

LAMB SHANK PIE

Serves 4
Here is another pie we often make which is similar to the lamb shoulder, but subtly different. Again, it does not have to be turned into a pie, just mash some potatoes and you have a meal.

4 lamb hind shanks
¼ cup flour
2 tablespoons light olive oil
1 big onion, peeled and cut into eighths
3 parsnips, peeled and cut into chunks
2 leeks, washed and cut into chunky rounds
2 whole bulbs garlic, tops almost cut off
6 bay leaves
2 stalks rosemary
¾ bottle red wine
1 litre chicken stock
1½ tablespoons cornflour
1½ tablespoons crabapple jelly
1½ teaspoons salt
freshly ground black pepper
2 sheets puff pastry
1 egg, beaten

Preheat the oven to 160°C.

Lightly dust the lamb shanks in the flour.

Place a large roasting dish across two hobs on a medium heat. Heat the oil, then add the onion and parsnips and cook until tender and lightly caramelised. Take out the vegetables and turn the heat up a little and quickly sear the shanks. Put the vegetables back into the pan along with the leeks, garlic bulbs, bay leaves and rosemary. Then pour in the wine and let it reduce by about a third. Now add the stock. Cover the dish with tin foil, sealing it well.

Put in the oven and cook very slowly until the meat is falling off the bones. This will take 3–4 hours.

When the lamb is cooked, remove from the oven and take the meat, garlic and parsnips out of the sauce. Put the dish with the remaining sauce in the fridge for half an hour, until the fat settles on the top and can be easily skimmed off.

When the meat is cool enough to handle, pull it away from the fat and bone. You should have lovely pieces of tender lamb.

Put the roasting dish with the sauce back on the hob and slowly heat it again. In a bowl, mix the cornflour with some of the sauce until it is smooth and then add this back

Continued over page

to the sauce. Add the crabapple jelly, salt and a jolly good grind of pepper. Squeeze the garlic cloves out their skins into the sauce. Stir until it comes to a gentle boil, then keep stirring until it starts to thicken, about 5 minutes. If there was not much liquid left after cooking the meat, just add some more wine and stock. Taste and adjust the seasoning. Add the meat and parsnips back into the sauce and mix it all together.

Preheat the oven to 200°C.

To make one big pie, pour the meat and gravy into a baking dish. Roll out the puff pastry on a floured bench until it is the size of the dish and place it over the meat. Brush the pastry with egg and press the edges with a fork to seal.

Put in the oven and cook until the pastry is done and the meat is bubbling up, about 40 minutes.

If you don't want to make a pie, serve the meat and vegetables folded though Potato Gnocchi (see page 78), or serve with mashed potato.

PARMESAN-CRUMBED LAMB CHOPS

Serves 4
These are the best. Children, grannies, adults, dogs . . . everyone wants these.

6 slices fresh bread
¾ cup grated Parmesan
½ cup flour
tiny pinch of salt
2 eggs, beaten
2 lamb racks, cut up into 16
    wee chops
2 tablespoons olive oil

Preheat the oven to 180°C.

Whiz the bread and the Parmesan together in a food processor until they are tiny breadcrumbs. Then fill one bowl with the flour seasoned with the salt, a second with the beaten egg and a third with the crumbs.

First dust the chops with the flour, then dip them in the egg, and then put them in the bowl with the crumb mixture, turning them until they are completely coated. If you want to make absolutely sure you have a lot of crumb on the chops, you can repeat the egg and breadcrumbs steps.

Lay the chops on a plate lined with greaseproof paper and put them in the fridge for at least half an hour to help set the crumbs.

Now you're ready to cook the chops. Place a large ovenproof frying pan on a medium heat and add 1 tablespoon of the oil. Brown the chops on each side. You will have to do this in batches, using the remaining oil. Then put them in the oven for 10–15 minutes to cook through.

These chops make great picnic food or they are lovely with Ratatouille (see page 192) and a roast vegetable or two, or with a salad or a big plate of blanched silverbeet dripping with butter.

OXTAIL STEW WITH GREMOLATA

Serves 4–6

It is great to see plates coming back to the kitchen where people have enjoyed the meal so much they have sucked every last bit of marrow out of the bones. This seems to be a dish filled with nostalgia; people remember their grandmothers making it. It is very simple, the meat has so much flavour it does all the work for you. At Pipi we sprinkle gremolata over the stew when we serve it. This is a mixture of lemon, garlic and parsley which is traditionally served with osso bucco (veal oxtail). Its strong flavours go really well with the richness of the meat. Oxtail is one of those dishes that tastes better the day after it is made, so it's great for a dinner party as you will have all that extra time on the day.

2.5kg oxtail

¼ cup flour

salt and freshly ground black pepper

2 tablespoons olive oil

4 slices bacon

2 medium-sized onions, cut into ½cm dice

7 cloves garlic, roughly chopped

1 carrot, cut into ½cm dice

2 sticks celery, cut into ½cm dice

2 cups white wine

2 x 400g cans whole peeled Italian tomatoes, crushed with a fork

6 bay leaves

Preheat the oven to 160°C.

Lightly dust the oxtail with flour seasoned with salt and pepper.

Next heat the oil in a big ovenproof dish on a medium heat. Cook the bacon until it is starting to brown, then take it out and set aside. Brown the oxtail all over on a low heat, in batches if you need to, and then take it out of the pan.

Then gently fry the onion, garlic, carrot and celery in the dish for about 10 minutes, or until they have softened and started to brown. Put the oxtail and the bacon back in the dish with the vegetables and add the wine. Reduce by just over half. Add the tomatoes and bay leaves to the dish. Now cover very tightly with a lid or with tin foil or both.

Put in the oven and cook until the meat is very tender and falls apart when you push it with a fork. This can take 4–4½ hours.

Continued over page

Gremolata

1 cup finely chopped parsley
½ cup finely grated lemon rind
3 cloves garlic, peeled and
  finely chopped

To make the gremolata, mix all the ingredients together well. Sprinkle on the oxtail stew when you serve it.

You need to serve the stew with something that will help soak up all the wonderful juices and complement the richness of the meat. Penne, mashed potatoes or parsnip or a simple risotto, which is also traditional with osso bucco, would all be great, along with something green.

BEEF AND STOUT STEW

Serves 4
This is full of flavour, just the thing for a cold winter's night.

1kg beef, cut into 1–1½cm
   cubes
¼ cup flour
2 tablespoons olive oil
10 pickling onions, peeled
50g pancetta, sliced into
   small strips
400ml stout
5 bay leaves
300ml mushroom stock
   (I use a good organic
   stock cube)
1 tablespoon seeded mustard
1 tablespoon soft brown
   sugar
1 dessertspoon good
   balsamic vinegar
20 whole green olives, pitted
3 sprigs of thyme
freshly ground black pepper

Preheat the oven to 160°C.

Lightly dust the beef cubes with flour.

Put the olive oil in a big ovenproof dish on a medium heat and add the onion. Cook the onions until soft. When they are almost done, add the pancetta and cook until it is just starting to brown. Now take the pancetta and onions out and brown the meat, in batches if you need to.

Now put the onion and pancetta back in the dish with the beef, pour in the stout and add the bay leaves. Turn up the heat and evaporate the stout a little. Then add the stock, mustard, sugar, balsamic vinegar, olives and thyme, and season with pepper. Cover the dish tightly with tin foil.

Put in the oven and cook for 2½ hours or until the meat is very tender. If a lot of liquid evaporates during cooking, just add some more stock.

This stew is delicious with rice and something green such as beans cooked and bathed in butter, a rocket salad or Brussels sprouts roasted and lightly dusted with grated ginger.

DUCK CONFIT

Serves 8

My childhood memories of duck are of rather tough wild muscovy duck, full of pellets from being shot. While these are happy memories, duck confit made using farmed birds is quite a different thing and very useful to have in the fridge at all times. Duck fat is traditional and delicious, but often hard to find and expensive. A light olive oil, like olive pomace oil, will do just as well; pomace is the oil extracted from the olive pulp after the first pressing.

9 cloves garlic, finely
  chopped
2¼ tablespoons flaky salt
8 sprigs of thyme, leaves only
8 duck legs
700g duck fat or 700ml light
  olive oil like olive pomace oil

Mix the garlic with the salt and thyme leaves. Then get a big container (plastic, not aluminium) and put a layer of the salt mixture over the bottom. Next add a layer of duck legs, skin side down, then cover the duck with more salt mix. Put another layer of duck on top of this, skin side up, then another layer of salt mix. Put in the fridge to do its thing for up to 24 hours. Next day, wash the salt mixture off the duck and dry well.

Preheat the oven to 80°C.

If using duck fat, put it into an ovenproof dish big enough to hold all the legs and place it in the preheated oven until the fat has melted. Now carefully drop the legs into the melted fat.

If using oil, put the duck legs into the dish and cover with the oil.

Put in the oven and cook for about 2½–3 hours or until the meat starts to come away from the bone and the duck is completely cooked. Make sure the liquid does not get any hotter than 80°C. The fat should just have little bubbles occasionally blipping up around the duck.

When the duck is cooked, sterilise a plastic container with boiling water and dry it. Then put in the legs and

Continued over page

completely cover with the hot oil or fat, making sure none of the duck is sticking out of the liquid. When the liquid has cooled, cover and seal the container. Now you can keep the confit in the fridge for up to 2 months — excellent, don't you think?

There are all sorts of things you can do with duck confit: fold it through a basic risotto with some Orange and Thyme Butter (see page 286) and spinach; break it up and have it with Potato Gnocchi (see page 78) and sage butter; make it into a sandwich with walnut bread, rocket and a creamy blue cheese; or serve it with Kumara Mash with Orange Zest and Thyme (see page 179), Caramelised Pear, Walnut and Rocket Salad (see page 181), or Watercress, Haloumi and Fig Salad (see page 190).

This is how we cook and serve Duck Confit at Pipi. Serves 4

4 legs Duck Confit (see page 132)

12 small potatoes, steamed and cut in half

100g Orange and Thyme Butter (see page 286)

4 tablespoons red wine jelly

Preheat the oven to 250°C.

Heat some of the duck fat or oil from the confit in an ovenproof frying pan on medium heat. Put the legs into the pan, skin side down. What you are doing is browning and crisping up the skin — it will not take long. Next put the cooked potatoes in the pan.

Place in the oven for 10–15 minutes until the duck and potatoes are warmed through.

Just before you've finished warming the duck and potatoes, put the orange and thyme butter and jelly on top of the duck legs. This makes a sauce as it melts, which you can pour over the duck and potatoes once they are on the plate.

CHICKEN CONFIT

Serves 2–3

I have always been haunted by a meal I had years ago in Italy. A local took me to a simple restaurant somewhere in Florence. There were no tourists and the food was amazing. We had tortellini in a clear broth, and then a chicken dish, which I have wanted to find the recipe for ever since, and, to finish, strawberries just picked from the hills around the city. Well, after years of pondering on the chicken I think I have cracked it — at least it comes close to the memory I have. Like the duck, this chicken would also be great in a sandwich or salad.

Quatre-épices spice mix
1 teaspoon ground nutmeg
1 teaspoon ground ginger
1 teaspoon ground cloves
2 teaspoons ground white
     pepper

1 teaspoon juniper berries,
     finely chopped
5 cloves garlic, finely
     chopped
¼ cup thyme leaves, finely
     chopped
1½ tablespoons flaky salt
1kg free-range chicken
     drumsticks
550g butter
2½ teaspoons Quatre-épices
     Spice Mix

For the spice mix, mix everything together.

Mix the juniper berries, garlic and thyme leaves together with the salt. Rub this mixture over the chicken drumsticks, then put them into a container that will not corrode. Place in the fridge for at least 12 hours and up to 24.

Preheat the oven to 100°C.

When ready to cook the chicken, wash off the marinade and dry the drumsticks with a paper towel.

Melt the butter slowly in a saucepan and then take it off the heat and stir in the spice mix. Place the drumsticks in an ovenproof dish that holds the chicken snugly, then pour over the butter mixture until they are completely covered.

Place in the oven and cook very slowly until the meat is falling off the bones, 2–3 hours.

Once it is cooked, remove from the oven and leave to cool in the butter. Next put the chicken into a clean, sterilised container and pour the butter over it so the chicken is fully submerged. Then cover the container and put it in the fridge until you want to use it. It will keep in the fridge for up to 3 weeks.

CHICKEN CONFIT WITH CABBAGE, CAVOLO NERO AND APPLE

Serves 4
This chicken is very rich, but delicious, and serving it with cabbage and cavalo nero helps to offset some of the richness.

1kg Chicken Confit (see page 136)

8 potatoes, skin on, cut in half and steamed

½ small cabbage, very finely sliced

300g cavolo nero, stalks removed, very finely sliced

1 tablespoon olive oil

1 green apple, peeled and finely sliced

2 teaspoons fresh thyme leaves

salt and freshly ground black pepper

Preheat the oven to 250°C.

Put the drumsticks into an ovenproof frying pan with a good amount of the surrounding butter. Add the cooked potatoes to the pan and place in the oven for about 10 minutes until the chicken is browned and the skin is crisp.

Meawhile, put the cabbage and cavolo nero in a colander and pour boiling water over it.

Heat the olive oil in a frying pan on a medium heat, add the apple and lightly brown. Then add the cabbage and cavolo nero, stirring together until the cabbage is just soft. Towards the end, throw in the thyme and season with a little salt and pepper.

Serve the cabbage mixture on the side of the chicken and potatoes.

POACHED WHOLE CHICKEN WITH TARRAGON

Serves 4

The idea of a delicately poached chicken with new potatoes and something green is a good one, don't you think? Very nurturing, very comforting and something you don't have to give too much thought to, but just do instinctively when you get the idea.

For the poached chicken

1 whole free-range size 22 chicken

1 leek, tough leaves discarded, cut into 2cm slices

2 stalks celery, cut in half

small bunch of parsley

small bunch of French tarragon

5 bay leaves

9 peppercorns

5 cloves garlic, peeled

For the potatoes and leeks

50g butter

¼ cup water

5 leeks, tough leaves discarded, washed and cut into 1cm slices

white pepper

12 new potatoes, skin on, washed

salt and freshly ground black pepper

For the chicken, put everything in a saucepan, cover the chicken with water, then very gently simmer until it is tender. This should take about 1½ hours depending on the size of your chook. You can tell when the chicken is cooked when the meat is tender and the juices run clear with no blood after pushing a knife into it.

Take the chicken out of the broth and keep warm on a serving plate. If you keep reducing the liquid for another hour, you will have a delicious stock to use for a risotto, soup or restorative broth.

For the leeks, melt the butter in a saucepan with the water and add the leeks, stirring them so they become coated with butter. Leave them to slowly melt — this will take about 40 minutes or so. Then taste and season with a little white pepper.

Steam the new potatoes until they are tender. Then put them onto the platter with the chicken and the leeks. Take it to the table to serve.

There are a few sauces that are good with the chicken: Salsa Verde (see page 289) or Lemon Mayonnaise (see page 290). Spoon these over the chicken or serve in a bowl for people to help themselves. Tarragon Butter (see page 286) is also good — place it on top of the chicken and potatoes while they are still warm.

140 / 141

Sunday Lunch

I love the idea of a long Sunday lunch. We always had them when I was a child, and my grandparents or friends of my parents would come. And later, when I went away to boarding school, on the rare occasions when I had been good enough to be allowed out after chapel on Sunday, my mother would always cook a huge lunch.

When you work nights, as we do, sitting down and eating a meal is not something you can take for granted, so making a big thing of weekend lunches is fun.

We usually have them in winter and lunch is normally something simple that you can do in your sleep: a roast with lots of vegetables and a comforting pudding.

Light the fire as soon as you get up and then turn on the oven in preparation for the lamb.

Meals like this are as much about the anticipation, so what better way to enhance this than to have the delicate smell of a lamb roast wafting through the house all morning.

Lamb can vary a lot in quality so make sure you buy it from someone you trust. For roasting slowly like this, you need to buy a leg with the bone in as it has much more flavour.

I will not give amounts as I have no idea how many you are having to lunch or how much they eat.

SUNDAY ROAST

To get the lamb leg ready for roasting, rub it with olive oil and then salt, then poke it all over with a knife and fill the cavities with peeled cloves of garlic. Put the lamb in a roasting dish along with 3 large sprigs of rosemary and a good glug of olive oil.

Place in the oven preheated to 160°C and let it slowly dissolve all morning. This will take about 4–5 hours depending on the size of the leg.

While the lamb is cooking, you can get the vegetables ready. Peel the potatoes and steam them until they are about half cooked. Cut up the cauliflower, so you have lots of little florets all about the same size, but not too small. Peel and cut some parsnips, lengthways. Wash some red onions, leaving the skin on, and quarter them. Make the Spinach Bake following the recipe on page 180. An hour before the meat is ready, put the parsnips and onion in with the meat, and turn them around in the juices.

In another ovenproof dish, splash in some olive oil and then add the potatoes. Shake them around so their edges get crushed — this makes them lovely and crunchy when they are cooked. Now put in the oven.

For the béchamel or white sauce for the cauliflower, melt 25g of butter in a saucepan on a low heat, then add 25g of flour and stir very well until they are completely mixed together. Keep cooking on a low heat for about 3–4 minutes, then pour in 500ml of milk and add 3 bay leaves. Keep cooking for another 5 minutes, stirring all the time. Continue cooking for another 10 minutes, but only stir every so often, by which time the sauce should have thickened.

When you are ready, steam the cauliflower and pile it onto a serving platter, then pour the white sauce over it.

When the meat is cooked, take the lamb and the vegetables out of the dish and put them on a big plate, keeping them warm while you make the gravy.

For the gravy, pour off most of the fat from the roasting dish, then, in a small bowl, mix 1 tablespoon of cornflour with ¼ cup of the cooking liquid from the meat (if there is not enough then use water). Pour this back into the dish and whisk to combine. Then add 1 cup of vegetable or chicken stock mixed with 1 cup of red wine and ¼ teaspoon of salt and 1 tablespoon of redcurrent jelly. Stir this around, getting all the nice bits from the bottom of the pan until the gravy has thickened nicely. A dash of marsala is also good.

Have a warmed gravy boat waiting for the gravy. As well as the gravy, mint sauce and crabapple jelly are very good with roast lamb.

Now pour everyone a glass of pinot noir and eat.

Next is pudding — Lemon Delicious is perfect.

LEMON DELICIOUS

½ cup sugar
1 tablespoon butter
2 tablespoons flour
pinch of salt
juice and zest of 1 lemon
1 cup milk
2 eggs, separated

Preheat the oven to 150°C. Grease a small ovenproof dish.

Beat the sugar and butter together, then add the flour, salt, lemon juice and zest, milk and egg yolks.

Beat the egg whites until stiff, then stir into the mixture and pour into the prepared dish.

Stand the pudding dish in a larger dish filled with hot water and place in the oven for about half an hour.

Serve with cream or ice-cream.

These are old friends
of pipi, they carry
her flag.

Carina Chambers, dear friend
pipi worker

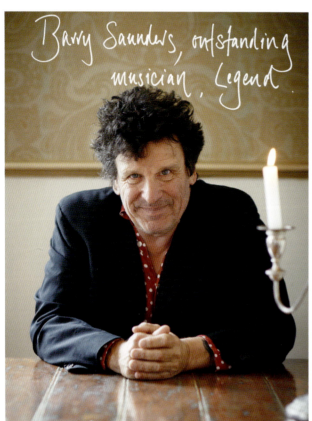

Barry Saunders, outstanding
musician, Legend.

Ant Vickerstaff, artist, pipi worker
wanderer

Dick Frizzell, famous artist

Tony Mills, old family friend pipi worker

Anna Rolman, greytown pipi worker, salt of the earth

Helen Furlong, fairy godmother

fish

BAKED WHOLE FLOUNDER

Serves 2
Since we first put whole flounder on our menu it has been one of our most popular dishes. For a lot of New Zealanders, it seems to bring back childhod memories of catching and eating flounder.

1 cup flour
1 teaspoon salt
2 x medium-sized whole
   flounder (500–600g each),
   gutted and cleaned
1 tablespoon olive oil
80g Caper Butter (see page
   286)

Preheat the oven to 250°C, or as high as it will go.

Season the flour with salt and scatter on a tray big enough to hold a flounder. Lay the flounder on top of the flour, making sure it gets a good dusting. Then turn it over and do the same with the other side. Repeat with the second flounder.

Oil a large oven tray with the olive oil and lay both flounder on top. Cover with tin foil and place in the oven.

After 9 minutes turn them over and put half the caper butter on top of each fish. Now put back in the oven, uncovered, until the butter softens and is starting to melt. This should only take another minute.

At Pipi, we serve the flounder with lemon wedges, roast potatoes and spinach blanched in a little water and lemon juice.

FISHCAKES WITH PEA AND BEAN PURÉE

Serves 4 (3–4 fishcakes per person)
The fishcakes at Pipi are traditional English-style ones, half fish and half mashed potato. The recipe can be changed and added to, but this is the basic version.

For the fishcakes
1kg potatoes, peeled
1kg white fish fillets, such as
    tarakihi or moki
1 litre milk
½ cup chopped curly-leaf
    parsley
½ cup chopped dill
¼ cup chopped capers
½ teaspoon salt

For the pea and
    bean purée
1½ cups Bean Purée (see
    page 295)
¾ cup cream
¾ cup frozen baby peas

Preheat the oven to 160°C.

Boil the potatoes, drain well and mash them until you have got out all the lumps. Then put them in a big bowl and set aside.

While the potatoes are cooking, place the fish in an ovenproof dish and cover with the milk. Put in the oven and poach very gently until just cooked, 5–8 minutes. Now drain the fish in a sieve.

Put the fish, parsley, dill, capers and salt into the bowl with the potatoes. The best way to mix all this together is with your hands, but if you don't want to do that, get a big spoon and very gently fold the ingredients into each other. What you are trying to do is mix them together without breaking up the fish too much. You still want to see bits of fish, however, if the fish pieces are too big the cakes will just fall apart when you cook them. Now shape the mixture into 70g balls, slightly bigger than an egg, and place in the fridge for at least an hour to settle and firm up so they are easy to cook.

Increase the oven temperature to 250°C.

We brown the fishcakes on the hob and then put them in the oven to heat through. Put a large ovenproof frying pan on a high heat and then add a good lug of oil. When the pan is nicely hot, but not smoking, add the fishcakes.

Continued over page

You can do this in batches if you want to. Gently move them around with a spoon, so they brown nicely all over. Now put the whole pan in the oven for about 10 minutes, which will give the fishcakes time to heat all the way through.

To make the pea and bean purée, put a saucepan on a medium heat. Add the bean purée, cream and peas, smashing up the peas as you heat the sauce.

Serve the fishcakes with the purée on the side.

VARIATIONS
Any of these variations would be good for breakfast with or without an egg.

SMOKED FISHCAKES
You can make the fishcakes with smoked fish as well, or even smoked eel would be good. Just substitute half of the white fish with smoked fish, which needs to be poached along with the white fish. Smoked salmon is also great in fishcakes. You could make up the 1kg of fish with, say, 400g of hot-smoked salmon and 600g of white fish — the hot-smoked salmon doesn't need poaching.

SALMON FISHCAKES
In fact, you could take out the white fish altogether and use salmon instead. To cook the salmon, brush it with olive oil and a bit of lemon juice and wrap it in tin foil. Then place in the oven preheated to 200°C until it is just cooked through, about 10 minutes. Potato is good with salmon, but so is kumara (I would use red kumara), so you could replace the potatoes too. I would not add parsley to the salmon fishcakes, just dill and capers. They would be good with a Spinach Purée (see page 180).

FISH STEW

Serves 6
I used to make this when I was the cook at the Clearview Estate winery restaurant one summer years ago. I had not done a lot of cooking in restuarants before and the owners Tim and Helma were very brave in taking me on. But I loved it, and I hope I did not cause them too much grief.

1–2 tablespoons olive oil
4 rashers bacon, cut into
    small strips
1kg potatoes, peeled and cut
    into big chunks
2 litres fish stock
100g butter
100g flour
400ml white wine, riesling
    would be good
500ml cream
1.5kg firm white fish fillets,
    cut into big chunks
3 cups cooked mussels
salt and white pepper
juice of ½ a lemon
small bunch of flat-leaf
    parsley, ripped

Put the oil in a big saucepan on a medium heat. Add the bacon and cook until starting to brown, then remove and set aside. Now put the potatoes in the saucepan, adding more oil if you need to. Stir for about 5 minutes or until starting to brown. Now add the fish stock and gently simmer until the potatoes are cooked, about 20 minutes. Then drain the potatoes, keeping the stock in a bowl to one side.

For the béchamel or white sauce, melt the butter in a medium-sized saucepan, then add the flour, stirring all the time until they are mixed together, about 3 minutes. Then add the wine, cream and 1 litre of the fish stock you cooked the potatoes in, and very gently cook, still stirring, for 15 minutes until the sauce has thickened a little.

Now return the big saucepan to a low heat and pour in the white sauce. Add the potatoes, bacon, fish and mussels. Gently simmer until the fish is just cooked, about 10 minutes. Season with salt and white pepper and add the lemon juice. Top with the parsley and there it is.

This is great with big chunks of thickly toasted bread rubbed with garlic and olive oil.

SMOKED FISH AND POTATO-TOP PIES

Makes 6 individual pies
This is real comfort food, nothing jarring or confronting, perfect for children and nursing mothers.

50g butter
50g flour
1 litre milk
4 bay leaves
1kg potatoes, a variety good
    for mashing such as Agria
    or Ilam Hardy, peeled and
    cut into chunks
25g butter
½ teaspoon salt
5 eggs
1kg smoked fish, such as
    blue cod or moki
handful of spinach, washed
juice of ½ a lemon
salt and freshly ground black
    pepper

Melt the butter in a saucepan on a gentle heat, then add the flour and stir continuously for 3 minutes. Add the milk and the bay leaves and keep stirring until the sauce starts to thicken, 4 minutes. Then cook very gently for 10 minutes, stirring occasionally. Take off the heat and cover with greaseproof paper until you are ready to use it.

Steam the potatoes until soft. Drain and put in a bowl along with the second measure of butter and the salt. Mash really well so there are no lumps.

Put the eggs in a saucepan of cold water and slowly bring to the boil. After 8 minutes take them out of the water and put under cold running water for 2 minutes. Then shell them and cut in half.

Break up the fish into bite-sizes pieces, discarding any skin or bones, and then fold the fish, spinach and boiled egg into the sauce. Add the lemon juice. Season with salt and pepper to taste. Smoked fish can be quite salty so you will need to make up your own mind about whether it needs more salt or not. You may want to add more lemon juice too.

Pour the fish mixture into 6 individual ovenproof dishes and spoon the mashed potato on top. You can put the pies in the fridge now if you want to cook them later.

Continued over page

Put a wee knob of butter on each one and into the oven. The pies should take about 20 minutes to warm through and for the potato to go crispy on top. The sauce will start bubbling up through the potato.

If you've made the pies ahead of time and had them in the fridge, you may need to cook them for longer. In this case you may need to cover them halfway through cooking so the tops do not get too brown.

If you do not want to make individual pies, just cook exactly the same but assemble it all in one big dish and cook for 20–25 minutes.

A green salad is the thing with these pies, and if you are a cider drinker, now would be the time to have a glass.

SALMON FILLET WITH RUM AND LIME

Serves 2

I have always liked teriyaki marinade for salmon and then when I tasted some Stolen gold rum it seemed that its lovely sweet, smoky flavour would also go very well with salmon, so here you are. I have tried this with Coruba as well and it is just fine.

½ cup Stolen gold rum or any other rum you have in the cupboard
2½ dessertspoons soft brown sugar
juice of 1½ limes
2 x 180g salmon fillets, skin on
salt
1 dessertspoon olive oil

Mix the rum, sugar and lime juice together and place the salmon in the marinade, skin side up, for at least 4 hours and not more than 12.

Take the salmon out of the marinade and pat it dry with a paper towel. Then sprinkle with a tiny bit of salt.

Heat the oil in a frying pan and put in the salmon, skin side down. Cook until the skin is lovely and crisp and then turn the salmon and cook for about 3 minutes more or to your liking. Take out the salmon and keep warm.

Pour the marinade into the pan with ¼ teaspoon of salt. Turn up the heat and let it reduce by about half or more, 3–4 minutes, then pour it over the salmon.

Serve with mashed peas and mint and celeriac roasted with ginger and then mashed.

WHITEBAIT FRITTERS

Makes 2 fritters

I did not grow up in a family that caught or ate a lot of whitebait. But Chris' family is from the West Coast of the South Island and through him I have got a sense of the whole tradition that surrounds whitebait. I have also come to eagerly await the beginning of each whitebaiting season. I think these fritters are best while still warm, sandwiched between two pieces of soft white buttered bread with lots of pepper and a squeeze of lemon. At Pipi, we serve them with Dill and Mint Mayonnaise (see page 290) and some rocket; either way, they are delicious.

20g flour

¼ teaspoon baking powder

¼ teaspoon salt

1 egg

70g whitebait

15ml New Zealand sparkling water

1 dessertspoon butter

1 tablespoon olive oil

Mix together the flour, baking powder and salt. Then beat the egg and add it to the flour, whisking the batter until it is smooth. Next fold through the whitebait and then the water.

Melt the butter with the oil in a frying pan on a medium heat. Cook the batter in two lots, so you have two fritters. When the fritter has cooked on the bottom, flip it over and cook it for another 2 minutes or until it is cooked through and slightly brown. It is easy to undercook the middle so a good way to check is to push lightly with your finger to see if there is any liquid still in the middle.

PAN-FRIED WHITEBAIT

My sons love whitebait for breakfast and rather than fritters, they like to eat them just very quickly pan-fried.

Melt some butter and quite a bit of oil in a pan, spread the whitebait out in the pan and sprinkle a pinch of semolina or flour over them, so they get lightly coated. Cook the whitebait on one side and then turn over for a few more seconds until they are slightly brown and crispy — it only takes a minute. Serve with a squeeze of lemon and salt and pepper.

Vegetables & Salads

POTATO TORTILLA

Serves 2–3

These tortilla are everywhere in Spain. They are usually served in the bars as tapas but they make a great lunch too. The trick is to not confuse them with frittata and to restrain yourself from adding little bits of red pepper or other vegetables. The glory of these is their simplicity and lots of olive oil.

¼ cup light olive oil
1 onion, peeled and sliced
3 big potatoes, peeled and
    cut into 3mm slices
4 eggs, beaten
1 teaspoon salt
½ teaspoon freshly ground
    black pepper

Heat 2 tablespoons of the oil in a smallish pan, about 20cm wide. Slowly cook the onion until it has softened completely, about 15 minutes. Put in a bowl with the uncooked potato slices and mix together. Put the mixture back in the pan, adding the rest of the oil. Really slowly cook the potatoes for about 30 minutes, turning them every so often so the slices on the bottom go to the top. Make sure they don't catch — covering the pan with a lid can help.

When the potato is cooked, pour it gently into a bowl with the eggs, salt and pepper. Mix carefully with a soft spatula so you do not break up the potato.

Return the pan to a low heat and pour the mixture back in. If there is not much oil in the pan, add some more — you don't want the tortilla to stick to the bottom. Now cook slowly until the egg is set everywhere except for the top middle. To cook this part you need to flip the tortilla. Loosen under and around the tortilla with a spatula. Find a plate that fits over the top of the pan, hold it there with one hand and with the other flip the pan. Your tortilla will flop onto the plate. Now you can easily slip it back into the pan and cook the other side. This only takes a few minutes; you only want to just cook it, otherwise it will be rubbery.

And there it is: done. Let the tortilla cool a bit as they are best just warm. Make a big green salad and you have lunch. They are also really good sliced and put between two pieces of good soft bread such as ciabatta.

KUMARA, ORANGE AND FENNEL BAKE

Serves 4 as a side dish
This goes really well with the Duck Confit (see page 132) or the Parmesan-crumbed Lamb Chops (see page 124). Kumara are a good source of vitamins A and C. I love them, and often have a wee stash of roast kumara in the fridge, as they make a great high-energy snack.

2 red kumara, peeled and chopped into quarters
1 fennel bulb, tough leaves discarded, washed and sliced lengthways into quarters
1 orange, skin on, sliced into 8 boats
1 tablespoon olive oil
1 cup water
½ cup maple syrup
pinch of salt and freshly ground black pepper

Preheat the oven to 180°C.

Put the kumara, fennel and orange into a well-oiled ovenproof dish and splash the olive oil over them. Mix the water and maple syrup together and pour over, turning the vegetables until they are well coated.

Sprinkle with the salt and pepper and cover the dish with tin foil or a lid.

Now put in the oven, and after 20 minutes take the cover off and turn the vegetables over, coating them well in the syrup. Then put back in the oven for another 20 minutes, or until the kumara and fennel are soft inside and nicely browned on the outside and the orange is caramelised.

ROAST VEGETABLE SALAD

Serves 6

Vegetables deserve just as much attention when they are being cooked as a prime cut of meat. Maybe because they are more forgiving, they do not always get it. But if you really think about how you are cooking and preparing vegetables, it makes a huge difference to how they taste. It is obviously up to you, but I have a strong opinion on how long vegetables should be cooked for. You do not want to overcook them, but undercooking is just as bad. I think a lot of people react against an upbringing of eating vegetables that were boiled to death by barely cooking them at all. They are missing out on the wonderful flavour that vegetables get when they have been cooked all the way through until soft and starting to caramelise. How far you take this is up to you. So here we go.

For the salad

2 carrots

3 medium-sized kumara

1 medium-sized parsnip

2 celeriac

1 small head broccoli, steamed

9 yams

½ small pumpkin

13 Brussels sprouts, outer
    layer peeled

2 red onions, peeled and cut
    into quarters

4 whole garlic bulbs, washed,
    with tops cut off

½ cup olive oil

For the dressing

½ cup extra virgin olive oil

1 tablespoon aged balsamic
    vinegar

¼ teaspoon salt

good grind of freshly ground
    black pepper

Preheat the oven to 180°C.

Wash, peel and cut the carrot, kumara, parsnip and celeriac into chunks about the same size, 3–4cm chunks, or rounds. Not too small, or they will just be oily and sad when cooked; and not too big or the dish would just be a little ridiculous and not a salad at all. Wash the yams. Cut up the pumpkin into the same size pieces, leaving the skin on, but getting rid of the pips.

Because all these vegetables cook at different times, to achieve the best result you need to cook them in different oven trays, except for the garlic and onion, which can share the same tray. Before putting all the vegetables on their separate oiled trays, mix them with your hands with a tablespoon of olive oil until they are well coated. You will need to turn the vegetables often during cooking, about every 10 minutes until they are done.

While the vegetables are roasting, make the dressing by giving all the ingredients a good shake in a sealed jar.

Continued over page

handful of flat-leaf parsley or
basil, ripped, to serve

Steam a head of broccoli. When the vegetables are cooked
to your liking, take them out and put them together in
a large bowl. Pour over the dressing, making sure all the
vegetables get thoroughly coated. The garlic with skins
on can go in as well — just squeeze the lovely caramelised
insides onto the other vegetables when you are eating the
salad. Sprinkle with the flat-leaf parsley or basil.

The dressing is great but the salad does not rely on it, so
if you want to skip the extra oil, just a squeeze of orange
juice and then some of the garlic squeezed out of its skin is
quite enough.

Put a portion in a bowl and go and sit on the grass under a
tree and eat it slowly.

VEGETABLE HASH

Nothing tastes more delicious than leftover vegetables mashed together and quickly pan-fried. Maybe it is a hangover from the puréed vegetables we were all fed for our first meals. Here are some combinations I like, but it is more an idea than a recipe.

COMBINATION SUGGESTIONS
carrot, parsnip and parsley
kumara, spinach and red onion
potato, garlic, cabbage and silverbeet
celeriac, cauliflower and pumpkin
peas, mint, potato and Brussels sprouts

Presuming the vegetables are all pre-cooked, mash them up. Some are better barely squashed with a fork so they still have lots of texture and you can taste the individual flavours, while others are better mashed to a smooth purée. Season the vegetables with salt and pepper, heat some oil in a pan and gently fry the mash until it starts to brown. Turn over a few times so the hash browns all over.

All of these vegetables are the sort of thing you would want to have with an egg and bacon for breakfast, or to eat with a perfectly cooked piece of steak.

KUMARA MASH WITH ORANGE ZEST AND THYME

Serves 4 as a side dish
This is good with Duck Confit (see page 132).

4 good-sized kumara, peeled and cut into medium-sized pieces
zest of 1 orange, cut into fine strips
2 sprigs of thyme, stalks removed
25g butter, melted
salt and white pepper

Steam the kumara, or if serving with duck confit, roast the kumara in some of the oil or fat from the duck.

Place the cooked kumara into a bowl along with the orange zest, thyme leaves and melted butter. If using the duck fat or oil, don't add the butter as it will be rich enough. Mash this really well with a potato masher, then finish it off with a wooden spoon until it's smooth and creamy. Season with salt and white pepper.

SPINACH PURÉE AND SPINACH BAKE

Serves 4 as a side dish
I always want to include this in a meal when I cook at home. You could use other leafy greens instead of the spinach if you want to, or a mixture of different greens.

SPINACH PURÉE

700g spinach leaves, washed
40g butter
¾ cup cream
¼ whole nutmeg, grated
¼ teaspoon salt
freshly ground black pepper

Bring a large saucepan of water to the boil and blanch the spinach for 2–3 minutes, or until it wilts. Drain, squeezing out as much water as you can.

Melt the butter in a large frying pan on a low heat and add the spinach. Cover with a lid and cook for about 6 minutes, stirring every 2 minutes. Now put the spinach in a blender, along with the cream and nutmeg, and purée until smooth. Simply season the spinach with the salt and a good grind of pepper.

Serve the purée as a sauce with salmon or roast vegetables, or bake it following the recipe below and it becomes a side dish which you can serve with whatever you wish.

SPINACH BAKE

Spinach Purée
2 eggs, beaten

Preheat the oven to 160°C.

Mix the beaten eggs with the spinach purée and pour into a lightly oiled ovenproof dish. Sit this dish inside a second larger dish, and pour boiling water into the larger dish so it comes three-quarters of the way up the side of the spinach dish (creating a bain-marie).

Place in the oven for 30 minutes or until the eggs have cooked. If the bake starts to go brown, cover it with tin foil. If you add some grated cheese at the same time as the egg, you have a simple lunch.

CARAMELISED PEAR, WALNUT AND ROCKET SALAD

Serves 4 as a side dish
An Autumn salad — great on its own, or with anything slightly gamey, such as duck, rabbit or deer.

1½ tablespoons butter
1 tablespoon walnut oil
3 pears, skin on, cut in half (don't bother coring them)
3 tablespoons caster sugar or honey
½ cup water
knob of butter
250g rocket
½ cup dry-roasted walnuts
salt and freshly ground black pepper

Preheat the oven to 180°C.

Heat a frying pan on a low heat, then melt the butter with the walnut oil to stop the butter burning. Put the pears into the pan, cut side down, and cook until they are golden brown. Next turn them over and sprinkle with the sugar or honey. Pour in the water and add the knob of butter.

Place in the oven and cook until soft, about 25 minutes. The longer you keep them in the oven, the more caramelised they will get.

Cover a platter with the rocket. Just before you are about to eat, place the pears on the rocket with the juice they have been cooking in and sprinkle over the walnuts.

Splash over some walnut oil mixed with salt and pepper.

SAVOURY SCONES

Makes 10 scones
These are so full of stuff they are more like a meal than a scone —
great for lunch (with maybe a poached egg on top). You can use lots of
combinations of vegetables and cheese; this recipe is just a guide. Don't
think of them as scones because they are quite different to others you may
have made. Cooking it in one big lot makes the scones very moist.

½ medium-sized squash
 pumpkin (500–600g), cut
 into wedges
3 cups flour
2½ teaspoons baking powder
120g Caramelised Onions
 (see page 293)
1 cup ripped spinach
1½ cups grated tasty cheese
1 cup milk
½ cup buttermilk
100g butter, melted
10 cherry tomatoes, halved

Preheat the oven to 180°C. Line a baking tray with
greaseproof paper and lightly grease.

Place the pumpkin in an oiled oven tray and roast until
really soft and golden, 30–35 minutes. When it is cooked,
scoop the flesh from the skin and break it up a little bit.

Put the flour, baking powder, Caramelised Onions,
spinach, pumpkin and almost all of the cheese in a bowl
and mix really well.

Combine the milks, add the melted butter, pour this into
the vegetable mixture and gently fold it in. It is important
not to overmix.

Spoon the scone mixture onto the prepared baking tray,
making one big scone about 3cm high. Sprinkle the rest of
the cheese over the top, and push the tomato halves, cut
side up, into the top of the scone.

Place in the oven and cook for 30–35 minutes. It is done
when a knife stuck into it comes out clean.

When it has cooled a little, cut it up into as many
individual scones as you want.

QUINOA, TUNA AND PURPLE POTATO SALAD

Serves 4 as lunch

Quinoa is excellent stuff. I often have it for breakfast either with avocado and tuna, or fruit and yoghurt. You could use fresh tuna in this recipe, but sometimes it is hard to find and there is nothing wrong with tinned.

For the salad

1½ cups white quinoa
1 cup good-quality tinned tuna
5 yams, washed
8 purple potatoes, scrubbed and chopped in half diagonally
¼ cup ripped radicchio
¼ cup toasted walnuts
½ cup chopped flat-leaf parsley

For the dressing

½ cup walnut oil
juice of 1 lemon
2 whole bulbs Garlic Confit (see page 294), crushed with a fork, or 3 fresh cloves, peeled and finely chopped
1 teaspoon runny honey
salt and freshly ground black pepper

Preheat the oven to 180°C.

Put the quinoa into a saucepan of boiling water and cook for 10–15 minutes until soft, then drain and set aside.

Put the yams in an oiled ovenproof dish. Place in the oven and cook for 15–20 minutes until soft.

Steam the potatoes.

Now tip the quinoa into a bowl along with the tuna, yams, potatoes, radicchio, walnuts and parsley.

Make the dressing by shaking all the ingredients together in a sealed jar. Pour the dressing over the salad. Next gently fold the salad all together with your hands, then spoon it onto a platter to serve.

A good loaf of bread and a lump of your favourite cheese and that is it: supper.

CAULIFLOWER AND ALMOND SALAD WITH ORANGE DRESSING

Serves 4
The size of the cauliflower florets is important — if they are too big they will just burn on the tips and not cook, and if they are too small they will just burn.

For the dressing
100ml extra virgin olive oil
juice of 2 oranges
1 dessertspoon Dijon
    mustard
½ teaspoon sugar
salt and freshly ground black
    pepper

For the salad
2 red onions, peeled and cut
    into wedges
1 particularly splendid
    cauliflower, cut into florets
    2cm wide
½ cup toasted almonds
small bunch flat-leaf parsley,
    ripped
1 tablespoon red
    peppercorns

Preheat the oven to 170°C.

First make the dressing, by putting all the ingredients in a sealed jar and shaking it up well.

Place the onion in an oiled oven tray and cook in the oven until soft and starting to brown, about 40 minutes.

Put the cauliflower florets on another oiled tray and into the oven for 20–30 minutes. Keep your eye on them and keep stirring — they need to be soft all the way through but not mushy.

Place the almonds on another tray in the same oven. You will also need to watch these as they burn easily.

When the cauliflower and onion are cooked, put them into a bowl and pour the dressing over straight away. Mix everything together gently so the vegetables get a good coating.

Spoon the salad onto a platter and cover with the almonds, parsley and red peppercorns.

It is tempting to add more to this salad and you could, I guess; but try to restrain yourself because I think it is good just like this.

LEMON ROASTED CHICKEN SALAD

Serves 4

We steam then roast the potatoes at Pipi, but the salad would also be just as nice with steamed new potatoes.

600g free-range skinless and
    boneless chicken thighs
1 tablespoon olive oil
1½ lemons, thinly sliced
4 potatoes, Agria are good
20 Kalamata olives
1 iceberg lettuce
2 good handfuls of rocket
couple of good pinches of
    flaky sea salt
12 Slow-roasted Tomatoes
    (see page 292)
½ cup extra virgin olive oil
2 dessertspoons aged
    balsamic vinegar
1 cup grated Parmesan

Preheat the oven to 180°C.

Put the chicken thighs in an ovenproof dish with the olive oil and lemon and cover with tin foil.

Place in the oven and cook for 15 minutes. Then take off the foil and put the thighs back for another 10 minutes or until they are done. Discard the lemon slices when the chicken is cooked.

Steam the potatoes until they're almost cooked. Drain and once they are cool enough to handle, cut them into quarters lengthways. Now put them into a small ovenproof dish with the olives, add a dash of good olive oil and cook in the oven for 15 minutes until brown.

Break the iceberg into clumps and lay it in the bottom of four bowls. Then place the rocket around and over it. Sprinkle over the sea salt and a splash of olive oil. Now put the potato, olives, slow-roasted tomatoes and the chicken on top and through the leaves.

Make the dressing by mixing the extra virgin olive oil with the balsamic vinegar and pour this over the salad. Then sprinkle the Parmesan on top.

WATERCRESS, HALOUMI AND FIG SALAD

Serves 4 as side dish
If you can't find a good aged balsamic vinegar, you are better to use a squeeze of orange juice in the dressing.

bunch of watercress, washed and well drained
8 perfectly ripe fresh figs
250g haloumi, cut into ½cm slices
2 tablespoons aged balsamic vinegar
¼ cup toasted hazelnuts, finely chopped
8 tablespoons extra virgin olive oil
¼ teaspoon salt
freshly ground black pepper

Preheat the oven to 180°C.

Place the watercress on a large platter. Cut the figs in half and put these on top of the watercress.

Put the haloumi slices in an oiled oven tray and cook in the oven for 10 minutes until golden brown.

Meanwhile, make the dressing by putting the balsamic vinegar, hazelnuts, extra virgin olive oil, salt and a good grind of pepper in a bowl and giving them a good stir with a fork.

Now spread the haloumi slices on top of the watercress and just before you are ready to serve, pour the dressing over the salad.

RATATOUILLE

Serves 4

This is a dish that just gets better and better the longer and slower it is cooked — and then you get to eat it. It makes a big difference if you brown all of the vegetables separately, because it means they maintain their individual flavours. If you have any old Parmesan rinds lying around in the fridge, this is a good time to pull them out. They add great flavour to the ratatouille. Just put them in with the tomato and let them dissolve into everything else. Make sure you fish out any that have not melted when the ratatouille is finished. While good on its own, it also works very well as a side dish with lamb or fish, or even toast a thick slice of bread, rub it with garlic and pour the ratatouille over the top.

2 tablespoons olive oil
1 big red onion, sliced not too finely
3 courgettes, cut on the diagonal into ½cm thick slices
2 red peppers, sliced into thin strips, discarding seeds and stalk
2 eggplant, sliced into 1cm rounds
8 cloves garlic, peeled and sliced
4 x 400g cans whole peeled Italian tomatoes
1 tablespoon white sugar or crabapple jelly
salt and freshly ground black pepper
bunch of basil, ripped

Add the olive oil to a big skillet and fry the onion slowly until it is completely soft and just starting to brown. Then take this out and cook the courgettes slowly until they are nicely browned on all sides. If you need to add more oil then do so. Take out the courgettes, then add the red peppers and cook on a low heat until they are soft and starting to brown. When they are done, take them out and add the eggplant — this guzzles oil so you will definitely need to add more. Cook these slowly until they are brown on both sides, then take them out.

Now add a little more oil and cook the garlic until it is golden and starts to smell amazing, then quickly add back the other vegetables, stirring them all together. Now pour in the tomatoes, squashing them so they release their juices. Stir through the sugar or jelly and cover with a lid, leaving it a little ajar.

Cook on a very low heat, stirring every 10 minutes. After an hour the vegetables will be cooked through and the sauce starting to reduce. At this point, you could season with salt and pepper to taste, throw the basil on top and say it is done. Or you could keep cooking and reduce it further. I would keep cooking for another hour or two until the tomato goes that lovely deep red and the flavours have all intensified.

Bar Food & Drinks

The Pipi Bar opened two days before Christmas in 2010. It is fun. We always felt we needed a place for people to wait for a table and there really was nowhere in our existing building, so when a space became available over the road it made sense to do it there. Hopefully it is the sort of place you can go to hide in for a while, either by yourself or with friends.

It is tiny inside with a larger space outside and yes, it is cold in winter but we have heaters, blankets and hot-water bottles to keep you warm.

Straight scotch is my drink of choice and I have never understood cocktails full of fizzy, fruity drinks in colours that could not possibly have come about naturally, crammed full of bells and whistles and umbrellas. But we found there was a demand for cocktails and when I started to research the classic ones, I realised they have a fascinating history. The search for the perfect martini, margarita or negroni can be addictive.

The bar is just Pipi, a little bit grown up; classic cocktails, local and Italian wine, champagne and, as well as taking over food from across the road, we have a small bar menu. Here is some of what we serve at Pipi Bar.

It is the idea of these cocktails and all the other classics that makes them important.

rted Sandwiches
a gruyere $9.90

ay biscuits
gorgonzola $14.90

ry bread
ts cheese &
en olives $14.90

queray & tonic $7.50

ari & Soda $7.50

m cup $8.50

hampagne cocktail

ellini $14.90

assic champagne
$1

rtini $14.90

queray 10 year
Martini $19.90

ojito $14.90

osmopolitan $14.90

n Fizz $14.90

egroni $14.90

argarita $14.9

CLUB SANDWICHES

Makes 16 or 32 sandwiches
Most people love club sandwiches, but there is a big difference between an exceptional one and a rather ordinary one. I usually make these for children's birthday parties; they are all you need to provide to keep the adults happy. Well, that and a glass of bubbly. (Adults are usually very happy eating the children's food anyway.) All of the sandwiches can be made up to two hours before serving. Just cover them with a damp teatowel or muslin and put them in the fridge. Take them out a little while before you want them as they are nicer not too chilled. So here are some ideas for fillings.

POACHED CHICKEN, TARRAGON MAYONNAISE AND CELERY

1 whole Poached Chicken (see page 140)
small bunch of French tarragon, chopped
1 cup Mayonnaise (see page 290) or a good store-bought one
24 slices white or brown sandwich bread
75g very soft butter
2 stalks celery, finely sliced
½ cup walnuts, very finely chopped
freshly ground black pepper

When the poached chicken is cool, pull good-sized pieces of meat away from the bones. Add the chopped tarragon to the mayonnaise.

Spread 8 slices of bread with mayonnaise and then place the chicken pieces on top. Very thinly spread some soft butter on another 8 slices and place these butter side down on top. Now cover the top of the second slice of bread with some mayonnaise, then sprinkle the celery and walnuts on top, and grind some pepper over. Next spread the last 8 pieces of bread with a thin layer of butter and put these butter side down on top of the celery and walnuts.

Now slice off the crusts and cut each sandwich into either two or four triangles, depending on what size you want.

Continued over page

EGG AND HAM

4 hard-boiled eggs
1 tablespoon cream
15g butter, melted
¼ cup finely chopped parsley
¼ teaspoon salt
freshly ground black pepper
24 slices sandwich bread, a
   mixture of white and brown
75g very soft butter
8 slices ham off the bone

Peel and mash the hard-boiled eggs very thoroughly with a fork. Then add the cream, melted butter, parsley, salt and a good grind of pepper. Stir to combine.

Spread 8 slices of bread with the egg mixture. Now spread the rest of the bread with butter. Take 8 slices and sit them on top of the egg butter-side up. Now lay the sliced ham on top and lay the remaining bread slices on the ham butter-side down.

Slice off the crusts and cut into either two or four triangles, depending on what size you want.

TUNA, WASABI MAYONNAISE AND ROCKET

1 cup Mayonnaise
   (see page 290)
15g wasabi paste
24 slices sandwich bread, a
   mixture of white and brown
1 cup good-quality tinned
   tuna
75g very soft butter
good handful of rocket

Mix the mayonnaise with the wasabi and spread it on 8 slices of bread. Place the tuna on the wasabi. Then very lightly butter the other 16 slices of bread and put 8 slices butter-side up on top of the tuna. Next put the rocket leaves on top of the buttered slices and then place the last 8 slices of bread butter-side down on top of the rocket.

Now slice off the crusts and cut into either two or four sandwiches.

HOT SMOKED SALMON, SORREL AND HORSERADISH CREAM

1 cup whipped cream
1 teaspoon caster sugar
2–3 tablespoons grated fresh
   horseradish
24 slices white or brown
   sandwich bread
700g hot smoked salmon
40g very soft butter
about 20 sorrel leaves

Mix together the whipped cream and sugar, adding enough horseradish until you are happy with the strength.

Spread 8 slices of bread with the horseradish cream and then place chunks of hot-smoked salmon on top to cover nicely. Then lightly butter 8 slices of bread and place these butter-side up on top of the salmon. Place the sorrel leaves on the buttered slices and then lightly spread a little more horseradish cream over 8 more pieces of bread and put these spread-side down over the sorrel.

Now slice off the crusts and cut into either two or four sandwiches.

SMOKED EEL PÂTÉ

Makes a bowlful, enough for a good-sized drinks party
You do not need much of this pâté as it is very rich. We serve it with
toasted Poesy Bread and it is also good with a grainy brown toast.

700g smoked eel
2 tablespoons chopped dill
½ cup chopped mint
1 cup crème fraîche
¾ cup cream cheese
juice of ½ a lemon
1 teaspoon green
    peppercorns

Pull the eel away from its skin and put it in a food
processor along with everything else except the
peppercorns. Process until the mixture is really well
blended and smooth. Then put in the peppercorns and
process for a little longer — you want the peppercorns to
still be a little chunky.

Now spoon the pâté into a bowl, sprinkle with a few more
green peppercorns, cover and refrigerate.

We serve individual portions in little paper cupcake
containers. This quantity fills seven cases.

TOASTED FLAT BREADS

We make a lot of these at our bar in the toasted sandwich machine. They are a great thing to have with drinks or for lunch. Here are some of the fillings we make and some other ideas. The good thing about tortilla or flat bread is the bread is so thin it becomes beautifully crisp and not at all heavy, so the flavours you fill them with really stand out.

COMBINATIONS

goat's cheese and plum paste
prosciutto and fresh mozzarella
ham and Gruyère cheese
Garlic Confit (see page 294), fresh mozzarella and basil
salmon, Salsa Verde (see page 289) and quark
aged cheddar and chilli flakes
green olives blended to a paste with chilli and brie

Just spread the fillings on one half of the bread and then fold the other side over the top. Brush the top with oil and also brush a little on the hot plate of the sandwich maker. Place the sandwich on the hot plate and squash down the lid. Keep checking until you are happy with how it's cooked — you want the fillings to be melting into each other and the bread to be golden brown and crisp. This will only take a few minutes. Take the sandwich out and cut it up into triangles or rectangles.

PAN-FRIED TOASTED SANDWICHES

Serves 2

We used to have these on the menu when we were open for breakfast, All sorts of fillings would work, but these are two we often made. They are like a mix between. French toast and a toasted sandwich, or a toasted sandwich that has been French toasted.

2 eggs
dash of milk
4 slices bread, you don't want
  the bread to be too thick

Filling 1
hot-smoked salmon
ricotta
Parmesan
spinach
Salsa Verde (see page 289)

Filling 2
2 slices champagne ham
2 slices Gruyère

1 dessertspoon olive oil

Whisk the egg and milk together in a large bowl. Make up the sandwiches with the filling of your choice, then dip them in the egg wash. Try to cover the whole sandwich.

Heat the olive oil in a frying pan on a low heat and put in the sandwiches. Cook for about 3 minutes or until the egg has cooked and browned, then turn them over and cook the other side in the same way. You also want to toast the bread and warm or melt the filling, so the pan needs to be on a low heat.

Better still you can put the whole pan in an oven preheated to 200°C after you have browned and turned the sandwiches once. If you have the time to do this, the sandwiches will really cook right through and puff up beautifully.

Take them out and cut in half. The cheese and ham ones are very good with Pipi Tomato Sauce (see page 90).

206 / 207

CLASSIC BELLINI

Venice is to me the most beautiful city in the world. A tiny piece of you stays behind when you leave, and you are left always feeling that something is not quite right. That is until the day you go back and you realise that you feel whole again. And of course I have been to Harry's Bar and tried the bellini and it is very touristy, but I don't care, the magic was still there. Make sure all of the ingredients are ice cold. For the purée, we mouli the peaches or use a mortar and pestle. Golden Queens are good.

$^2/_3$ glass good méthode champenoise or prosecco
$^1/_3$ glass peach purée

Fill a chilled champagne flute or saucer two-thirds full with bubbly. Now top with the peach purée.

NEGRONI

Strong and to the point, a negroni is perfect after a crazy night at Pipi.
By the time you have finished it you are asleep.

30ml good gin
30ml Campari
30ml Martini Rosso
slice of orange, to serve

Measure the ingredients into a mixing glass. Now pour into a cocktail shaker filled with very cold ice, and stir gently. Strain into your favourite large crystal tumbler, two-thirds filled with ice and 1 thin slice of orange.

MARTINI

This is the drink that everyone has a very strong opinion about — it is either too watery, or the olives were not right, and so on. But rather than putting me off, this has made me rather respect this drink and determined to make the perfect martini.

1 stuffed green olive
60ml very nice gin
splash Noilly Prat dry white
   vermouth or other dry white
   vermouth

First chill a martini glass, then put a toothpick through a stuffed green olive and keep it handy. Now pour the gin into a mixing glass, adding just the smallest splash of Noilly Prat. Next fill a cocktail shaker with the coldest ice you can find (go for the white frosty cubes and try not to use any half-melted ones).

Pour the gin and vermouth over the ice and stir gently about nine or ten times until the drink becomes very, very cold. Now strain into the chilled martini glass and add the olive.

Pudding

APPLE CRUMBLE

Serves 4–6

This is a classic crumble and it reminds everyone of the pudding their grandmother used to make. The trick here is not adding anything else. Crumbles made with polenta and almond meal are great, but your grandmother would probably not have made them like that. Also, I can never bring myself to mix fruit: if you are going to make an apple crumble then don't add berries or rhubarb to it. The pure taste of just one type of fruit is what makes it comforting and nurturing. Braeburns are great in crumble; Granny Smiths are also good because they're not too sweet — use them if you want a stewed look because they mush up when cooked.

2kg cooking apples, peeled, cored and cut into ½cm thick slices
½ cup caster sugar
1¼ cups flour
1¾ cups whole rolled oats
¾ cup soft brown sugar
2 teaspoons baking powder
250g butter, melted

Preheat the oven to 160°C.

Put the apple in a saucepan with quarter of a cup of cold water, sprinkle in the caster sugar and cook until soft. You will need to cover it for a while at first and stir often.

Mix the other dry ingredients together in a bowl and then pour in the melted butter.

Drain the apples and put them in a baking dish. Now spoon the crumble over the top, don't push it down flat.

Cook in the oven for 1 hour until the crumble is completely cooked and golden brown.

Serve with cream or ice-cream.

TIRAMISU

Serves 6–8
Very delicious and not at all hard to make, tiramisu is for me about the coffee. At Pipi we perfectly extract espresso shots until we have two cups worth. But if you do not have an espresso machine, you can do it just as well with a plunger or a stove top. The important thing is that the coffee is not bitter or the whole tiramisu will be. Assemble this in a deep bowl, with 10cm high sides, which holds roughly 2–3 litres.

200g caster sugar
5 egg yolks
500g mascarpone
60ml sweet marsala
2½ cups cream, whipped
2 cups coffee
2 tablespoons caster sugar
90ml sweet marsala
about 650g sponge fingers
   (2½ x 250g packets)
grated dark chocolate or
   Dutch cocoa for dusting

Put the sugar and egg yolks in a bowl and whisk a bit so they are blended. Put this bowl over a saucepan of simmering water; you do not want the bowl to touch the water. Start whisking again until the mixture becomes thick and creamy.

Mix the mascarpone and first measure of marsala into the eggs and sugar. Then fold in the whipped cream.

Mix together the coffee and the second measures of sugar and marsala.

To assemble the tiramisu, dip the sponge fingers into the coffee-marsala mix. Now it is important how you do this. If they are too soggy, you will get a pool of the coffee mixture at the bottom of the tiramisu and if they are too dry, the tiramisu be dry too. So it is really just in and out — it is not as hard as I have made it sound and practice makes perfect.

In the deep-sided bowl, first cover the base with a layer of coffee-marsala-soaked fingers. Then cover this with a layer of the cream mixture. Alternate until you reach the top. Make sure you finish with a cream layer.

Lastly, dust with either chocolate or cocoa.

STICKY DATE PUDDINGS

Serves 6
These are very popular at Pipi. Once or twice I have tried to take them off the menu, but we are always persuaded to put them back on.

180g dates
85g prunes
300ml water
1 teaspoon baking soda
75g butter
150g soft brown sugar
2 eggs
1 cup flour
3½ teaspoons baking powder
120g dark chocolate (70% cocoa solids), chopped into bits no smaller than your fingernail (or they will melt completely)

Preheat the oven to 180°C. Line six of the cavities in a muffin tin with greaseproof paper so the paper comes 3cm over the top of the tin, creating a much bigger container for the mixture, which means you get bigger puddings.

Put the dates, prunes and water in a small saucepan and bring to the boil. Take off the heat, add the baking soda and then blend well in a whiz.

Now cream together the butter and sugar with an electric beater. Add the eggs one at a time.

In a separate bowl, mix the flour and baking powder together. Then fold this and the chocolate into the creamed butter and sugar. Add the date and prune mixture.

Fill each muffin cavity three-quarters full. Put in the oven and cook for about 30 minutes or until just done. You want them to be still a bit squishy, but not runny.

Serve with Caramel Sauce (see page 224).

At Pipi if we're not serving the puddings immediately and they need to be reheated, we put ½ cup of cream in a saucepan with a pudding, cover it and put the pan in a very warm oven. Once the pudding is warm through we take it out, cover it with the caramel sauce and warm cream, and there you are.

Continued over page

STICKY DATE CAKE
The date pudding recipe also makes a great cake.

Just make the recipe in the same way but double it and instead of cooking it in muffin tins, line two 30cm x 22cm shallow cake tins with greaseproof paper (make sure the paper goes well above the side of the tin) and fill them each three-quarters full of the mixture.

When they are cooked, remove from the oven. Because the cakes are quite soft, it is best to leave them in the tins until almost cool. Put one cake on a plate and spread some of the caramel sauce mixed with whipped cream over the top of it. Then put the other cake on top of this and, if you want to go all out, pour more caramel sauce over the whole cake.

224 / 225

CARAMEL SAUCE
Making this sauce can be tricky, and I admit that it took me ages to perfect without crystallising the sugar. But I think it is all about confidence and having a very clean heavy-based saucepan. And apparently also not stirring helps. Also helpful is using a clean pastry brush to push any of the liquid that shoots up the sides of the pan back down into the rest of the sauce.

440g caster sugar
½ cup water
80g butter
160ml cream

Mix the caster sugar and water in a saucepan on a gentle heat. Bring to the boil and cover for 3 minutes, then remove the lid and gently boil until it becomes a deep caramel colour. Once this happens, quickly remove from the heat and whisk in the butter and cream.

This sauce is also wonderful with ice-cream and baked pears.

STRAWBERRY SHORTCAKE

Serves 6–8

This is my mother's recipe. We had pudding most nights and this was one of my favourites. You can make it with any fruit; we also use feijoas, apricots, peach, apples or tamarillos. You will need 1.5kg of fruit and you'll have to cook it first. Peel fruit if necessary and cut in half. Then poach in a little water and ⅓ cup of sugar if you are using a sour fruit, until just soft. Let the fruit cool a little before you use it. The pastry is soft so do not worry if you have trouble rolling it out.

1¼ cups flour
1 cup caster sugar
1 teaspoon baking powder
120g butter
1 egg, beaten
1.5kg strawberries, washed
  and hulled
⅓ cup caster sugar
icing sugar for dusting

Preheat the oven to 160°. Grease a 20cm round dish.

Mix the flour, sugar and baking powder together in a bowl. Cut up the butter and rub it with your fingertips into the dry ingredients until the mixture looks like breadcrumbs. Then add the beaten egg. Bring it all together with your hands until the ingredients are mixed together, handling as little as possible or the pastry will become tough.

Cut the pastry in two and roll out one half on a floured bench until it is the size of the dish. Now line the greased dish with the rolled-out pastry. Fill it with the strawberries, keeping them whole if possible. Sprinkle with the second measure of caster sugar.

Roll out the other half of the pastry and put it over the strawberries. The pastry is quite soft and often you end up putting it on in pieces, but it works out fine in the end.

Put in the oven and bake for 1 hour or until the shortcake is golden. You may need to cover it with foil during this time if the top starts to get too brown.

Dust with icing sugar and serve with cream or ice-cream.

RICE PUDDING

Serves 4
It seems a lot of people have had a bad experience with rice pudding,
but do try this and hopefully it will be a revelation.

90g Arborio rice
85g caster sugar
1.7 litres full-cream milk

Preheat the oven to 160°C. Grease an ovenproof dish with butter.

Mix the rice, sugar and milk together in a bowl, then pour it into the dish.

Put in the oven and cook very slowly for 3–4 hours. What you are doing is caramelising the sugars. You will need to stir often and scrape down the sides. The pudding is ready when it has gone a lovely dark golden colour.

This is delicious with strawberries cooked in sugar until they are almost like jam, or stewed rhubarb, feijoas or prunes.

CROISSANT BREAD AND BUTTER PUDDING

Serves 6

I have horrific memories of bread and butter pudding from school days, but this one has completely dispelled them. It is great for breakfast. If you have friends staying, why not get up early and whip this into the oven.

8 croissants, sliced in half horizontally
75g butter, softened
200g dates
9 eggs
4 egg yolks
120g caster sugar
450ml milk
750ml cream
icing sugar for dusting

Preheat the oven to 180°C. Grease a large ovenproof dish with butter.

Brush the croissants lightly with the softened butter. Lay all of the bottom halves of the croissants cut-side up on the base of the dish. Then rip up the dates over the croissants. Put the tops of the croissants over the dates.

Whisk the eggs, egg yolks and sugar together, then add the milk and cream and pour this over the croissants. Let it stand for 10 minutes so it all has time to settle in together.

Put in the oven and bake for 35–40 minutes. Then take it out, cover with tin foil, and return to the oven, cooking for another 40–50 minutes or until the custard is just set. Dust with icing sugar to serve.

You don't need anything with this, except maybe a dash of whipped cream, or lots of coffee if it's breakfast.

CHERRY CLAFOUTIS

Serves 6

This is a great pudding; everyone gets excited when the cherries pop up and this is a very appropriate way of using them. You can, and probably will, make it at other times of the year with other fruit, and that is none of my business, but it is best with cherries.

90g flour
3 eggs
3 tablespoons caster sugar
400ml milk
600g cherries, pitted
icing sugar for dusting

232 / 233

Preheat the oven to 170°C. Grease an ovenproof dish.

Sift the flour into a bowl with the eggs and the sugar. Beat these with a whisk until you have a smooth batter. Then add the milk and the cherries and pour into the dish.

Put in the oven and cook for 45–60 minutes or until just set. You will know it is cooked when the clafoutis is puffy and golden, and when a knife poked into it comes out clean.

When at room temperature, dust with icing sugar and serve with whipped cream.

BAKED CHEESECAKE

Serves 6–8

A classic cheesecake with a pastry base is a lovely thing. They seem to have gone out of fashion but I think it is time they came back. The pastry recipe comes from Moise Cerson from the French Baker in Greytown and Ya Bon in the Hawke's Bay. If you don't like sultanas, don't put them in. Instead add the finely grated zest of a big lemon. The butter, cream cheese and the eggs need to be at room temperature, so get these out of the fridge 30 minutes before you start.

For the pastry

200g unsalted butter, cut into cubes and at room temperature
200g icing sugar
2 eggs, lightly beaten
pinch of salt
400g flour
½ teaspoon baking powder
1 egg white

For the filling

750g cream cheese, at room temperature
180g sour cream
180g cream
4 eggs, at room temperature
1 dessertspoon vanilla essence
140g icing sugar
1½ tablespoons cornflour
½ cup sultanas

Beat together the butter, sugar, eggs and salt in the bowl of an electric mixer until combined.

Mix the flour, baking powder and salt together. Pour it into the mixer bowl with the butter mixture. Mix as quickly as possible — the less it is handled the better. Take it out and gently push it into a disc shape, wrap in baking paper and put in the fridge for 1 hour.

Preheat the oven to 180°C. Grease a 20cm springform cake tin.

Take out the pastry and cut off a third. Wrap this up again and refrigerate. Then, on a cold, floured bench, roll out the rest of the pastry to fit the bottom and sides of the tin.

Line the tin with the pastry, and then cover the pastry with greaseproof paper. Now tip in rice or dry chick peas to weigh it down. Make sure you cover all the pastry or it will go very brown on the edges.

Now put in the oven and bake for 10–15 minutes. Then take it out and tip out the weights. Brush it with egg white and put back in the oven to cook for another 5 minutes. Take out and cool.

Reduce the oven temperature to 160°C.

Continued over page

Mix all the filling ingredients except the sultanas together in a cake mixer until smooth. Scatter the sultanas over the base of the cooked pastry case, then pour the filling mixture on top.

Now roll out the rest of the pastry on a cold, floured bench. Cut it into strips and make a lattice pattern on top of the cheesecake.

Place in the oven and cook slowly for 1 hour. Try not to look at the cheesecake for a while as opening the door may make it crack. But you will want to check that the top is not getting too brown, so after about half an hour — if it starts to brown, cover with tin foil. You want the cheesecake to still have a bit of a wobble, as it will keep cooking for a while after you take it out of the oven. Cool completely in the tin before turning it out. This will take about an hour.

This cheesecake does not need much with it, maybe just a glass of sauternes.

FRUIT SPONGE PUDDING

Serves 4

There are people who don't eat pudding, others who like a light cold something, and then there are those of us who like puddings to be nurturing, warm and maybe even a little stodgy. In which case this pudding is perfect. You can make it with lots of different types of fruit; gooseberries are particularly sour so they need the sugar when cooking. Sweeter fruits will not need as much sugar.

1kg gooseberries, topped and
    tailed
200g caster sugar
¼ cup water
150g butter, softened
150g caster sugar
2 eggs
¼ teaspoon vanilla essence
150g flour
2 teaspoons baking powder

Preheat the oven to 180°C.

Put the gooseberries in a saucepan with the sugar and water. Stew away for about 10 minutes until the fruit is soft.

Beat the butter and sugar together in a bowl until it is nice and creamy. Add the eggs and beat a little more. Then add the vanilla. Mix the flour with the baking powder and fold it into the creamed mixture.

Drain most of the water from the gooseberries and then pour them into the dish you are going to cook the pudding in. Any ovenproof dish that holds enough pudding for four portions will do. Next spoon the topping over — don't pat it down, you want it to look like it can breathe.

Put in the oven and cook for 40–45 minutes. If the top gets too brown during this time, cover it with some tin foil. You will know it is cooked when a knife poked in comes out clean.

CARDAMOM PANNACOTTA, ROASTED PEARS AND GINGER

Makes 6 individual puddings

Pannacotta are great when you just want a light pudding after a substantial main course. I have made this with two sheets of gelatine and it set, but only just, so it is up to you. If you want to take them out of the moulds and definitely hold their shape, well then, use three sheets. But if you don't mind about any of that and prefer a lighter, softer set then use two.

For the pannacotta

2 or 3 sheets gelatine
500ml cream
100ml full-cream milk
100g caster sugar
10–15 cardamom pods, crushed to get 1 dessertspoon of seeds

For the roasted pears

3 tablespoons butter, melted
½ cup soft brown sugar
3 pears, cut in half and cored
½ cup thinly sliced fresh ginger

For the pannacotta, first soak the gelatine in a little cold water.

Gently heat the cream, milk, sugar and cardamom seeds until just boiling and then very gently simmer for 5 minutes. Take off the heat. Strain the cream mixture through a sieve.

Squeeze all the water out of the gelatine and stir it into the cream mixture until it dissolves. Pour into 6 moulds or tea cups and put in the fridge to set. This will take about 4 hours.

Preheat the oven to 180°C.

For the rosted pears, put the butter in an ovenproof dish, then sprinkle the sugar on top. Place the pears cut-side down in the sugar. Now place the ginger around them.

Place in the oven and cook for about 20 minutes, then turn the pears over and cook for about another 10 minutes until tender.

Continued over page

To serve, sit each pannacotta in a saucer of very hot water. This will loosen them so they are easy to unmold, but you may still need to run a knife around the edges.

Unmold each one onto a pudding plate and place a pear half next to it. Then spoon over some of the roasting juices.

CHOCOLATE ICE-CREAM

Make 4 litres
Very rich, very delicious; the vodka helps the ice-cream stay soft and stops it from becoming icy. Basically a good ratio for ganache is three to one chocolate to cream; this will set hard enough to ice fudge or cakes.

For the chocolate ganache
Makes 4½ cups
750g dark chocolate (70% cocoa solids), chopped
250g cream

For the ice-cream
9 eggs
3 cups caster sugar
900ml cream, whipped to soft peaks
3 tablespoons vodka
4½ cups chocolate ganache

For the ganache, put the chocolate and cream in a bowl over a saucepan of boiling water, making sure the bowl does not touch the water. Let them slowly melt together. I always take the bowl off the heat when some of the chocolate is still solid and then stir it until it has completely melted.

For the ice-cream, beat the eggs with the sugar until creamy, about 4 minutes. Gently fold the egg and sugar mixture into the whipped cream, add the vodka, and then fold through the just-warm ganache. It is important the chocolate is not too hot, but it has to be slightly warm or it will be too hard to mix in.

When it is all mixed together, pour into a container and freeze. It will be about 4 hours until the ice-cream is ready to eat.

GINGERBREAD ICE-CREAM

Makes 1 litre
This is the best.

100g Gingerbread (see page
    256), thinly sliced
¾ cup soft brown sugar
1 teaspoon ground ginger
4 eggs, separated
110g icing sugar
430ml cream, whipped

Preheat the oven to 80°C. Line a baking tray with greaseproof paper.

Dry out the gingerbread in a warm oven for 2 hours until crisp. Remove and set aside.

Meanwhile, melt the brown sugar and ginger in a saucepan on a low heat. You will need to stir this all the time so it does not burn. Just as it is becoming liquid, pour it onto the greaseproof paper. Straight away break up the gingerbread over the top of the sugar. Once the sugar has cooled and set, put it in a food processor and blitz it into small chunks.

Beat the egg whites until they form soft peaks and then add the icing sugar and beat a little bit more. Next beat the egg yolks until creamy and then fold the beaten egg yolks and whipped cream together with the egg whites and caramelised gingerbread chunks.

Pour this into a plastic container and put in the freezer. It will take about 5 hours to freeze.

ROSE PETAL ICE-CREAM

Makes 2 litres
This has a lovely delicate flavour. If you want it to be stronger just
add more rose water.

For the sugar syrup
1 cup caster sugar
½ cup water
2½ teaspoons rose water

For the ice-cream
8 egg yolks
600ml cream, whipped
½ cup dried rose petals

For the sugar syrup, put the sugar, water and rose water in
a saucepan and bring to the boil. Let it boil away for about
8 minutes or until there are even-sized small bubbles
all the way across the syrup. Cool completely. This is
important: if it is not absolutely cold, the cream will
separate when added.

For the ice-cream, beat the egg yolks in an electric mixer
until very pale and thick. Slowly add the sugar syrup to the
eggs. It will rise up a lot so use a big bowl. Then fold in the
whipped cream. Lastly, add the dried rose petals.

Pour into a plastic container and put in the freezer. It will
be about 5 hours before you can eat the ice-cream.

BROWN BREAD ICE-CREAM

Makes 1 litre
This may sound a little odd, but trust me it is delicious.

1 cup grainy brown bread
    crumbs, such as Vogels
¾ cup soft brown sugar
4 eggs, separated
110g icing sugar
430ml cream, whipped

Mix the bread crumbs with the brown sugar. Then put it in a saucepan on a low heat to caramelise. If the mixture starts to catch, add a few drops of cold water. Cool the bread mixture, then whiz it up in a food processor into small chunks.

Beat the egg whites until they form soft peaks and then add the icing sugar and beat a little bit more. Next beat the egg yolks until creamy and fold the whipped cream together with the egg whites and caramelised bread chunks.

Pour this into a plastic container and put in the freezer. It will take about 5 hours to freeze.

Cakes & Biscuits

OAT BISCUITS

Makes 25–30
These biscuits are good with cheese; we serve them with Gorgonzola and a fruit paste.

125g butter, softened
30g caster sugar
1 egg
1½ cups flour
1 teaspoon baking powder
1½ cups rolled oats

Preheat the oven to 180°C. Line a baking tray with greaseproof paper.

Cream the butter and sugar until light and creamy. Then add the egg and beat the mixture all together.

Now sift the flour and baking powder into another bowl, then add the oats. Stir the wet mixture into the dry, then knead it with your hands until it forms a nice ball.

Lightly flour a bench and roll out the dough until it is about ½cm thick. Now cut it into rough rectangles. Slide the biscuits onto the baking tray.

Put in the oven and bake for 15–20 minutes. The biscuits are ready when they are light brown and cooked through.

Cool on the tray for a few minutes before cooling completely on a wire rack. They will keep for 2–3 days.

LIME AND WHITE CHOCOLATE BISCUITS

Makes about 12 biscuits
If you like chocolate chip biscuits, you have to try these.

For the biscuits

125g butter
¼ cup sugar
3 tablespoons condensed
  milk
½ teaspoon vanilla
1½ cups flour
1 teaspoon baking powder
¾ cup white chocolate, cut
  into chunks
3 drops lime oil

For the icing

250g white chocolate
knob of butter

Preheat the oven to 170°C. Line a baking tray with greaseproof paper.

For the biscuits, cream the butter, sugar, condensed milk and vanilla together until thick and creamy. Mix the flour and baking powder together, then fold into the butter mixture, along with the chocolate and lime oil.

Next roll the biscuit mixture into balls and put them on the tray. Squash them with a fork but don't make them too flat.

Put in the oven and cook for about 15 minutes or until just lightly golden.

Remove from the oven and cool on the tray for a few minutes before cooling completely on a wire rack then icing.

For the icing, melt the chocolate with the butter in a bowl over simmering water, making sure the bowl doesn't touch the water. Take off the heat and cool. When the icing has cooled, spread it over the top of the biscuits. You could finely grate some lime zest over them as well, if you are in that sort of mood.

The biscuits will keep for 2–3 days.

GINGERBREAD

Makes 1 large or 2 small loaves
Everyone loves gingerbread and this one, which is from the Waihi School cookbook *Fuel for your Family*, is particularly good. At Pipi we serve this toasted with crème anglaise or cream. It is also good warmed and buttered, with a cup of tea.

2 cups flour
1 cup soft brown sugar
1 teaspoon baking powder
1 teaspoon baking soda
2 dessertspoons ground
    ginger
½ teaspoon mixed spice
½ teaspoon nutmeg
1 teaspoon cinnamon
250g butter
1 cup golden syrup
3 eggs, lightly beaten
1 cup milk
icing sugar for dusting

Preheat the oven to 160°C. Grease two loaf tins and line with greaseproof paper.

Sift the dry ingredients into a large bowl.

Melt the butter and golden syrup together.

Add the eggs to the dry mixture, followed by the butter and golden syrup, and the milk. Mix together and pour the batter into the loaf tins.

Put in the oven and cook for 50– 60 minutes, or until a knife poked in the centre comes out clean.

Cool in the tins for 10 minutes then turn out onto a wire rack. It will keep for 3–4 days.

CHOCOLATE CAKE

Serves 10

A simple and not too rich chocolate cake, this would work just as well made in muffin tins to produce small cakes. We make it in a rectangular tin, cut it in half and then slice these halves in half sideways so we have four flat pieces which we layer with berry purée and chocolate ganache. Because we have an espresso machine, we make the cup of coffee by layering perfectly extracted shots, one on top of the other. This makes it very strong, so if you are using plunger coffee, you could use two cups of coffee instead of one water and one coffee.

2¾ cups flour
1 cup cocoa
½ teaspoon baking powder
2 teaspoons baking soda
4 eggs
2½ cups caster sugar
1 cup water
1 cup strong coffee
1 cup vegetable oil
1½ teaspoons vanilla essence

Preheat the oven to 170°C. Line a 22cm x 32cm cake tin with greaseproof paper.

Sift the flour, cocoa, baking powder and soda together. Beat the eggs lightly with the sugar, and then add the water, coffee, oil and vanilla. Fold the wet ingredients into the dry and stir until they are well combined. Pour the mixture into the tin.

Put in the oven and cook for 30 minutes or until a knife poked in the centre comes out clean.

Remove from the oven and cool for a few minutes in the tin before turning out onto a wire rack. Then ice with Chocolate Ganache (see page 264), when completely cool.

STRAWBERRY JAM SPONGE ROLL

Serves 8
I love the idea of a simple sponge cake with cream and strawberries.
Making it into a roll is just more fun.

5 eggs, separated
$^2/_3$ cup caster sugar
1 teaspoon vanilla essence
pinch of salt
$^2/_3$ cup flour
4 tablespoons butter, melted
  and cooled
icing sugar for dusting
1 cup cream, whipped
1 small punnet strawberries,
  hulled and roughly
  chopped

Preheat the oven to 180°C. Grease a Swiss roll tin and line it with greaseproof paper.

Beat the egg yolks until really thick and creamy, then gradually add all but 2 tablespoons of the sugar. Next add the vanilla and keep beating for another 2 minutes. Beat the egg whites in another bowl with a wee pinch of salt until they form soft peaks, then add the remaining 2 tablespoons of sugar and beat to stiff peaks.

Sift the flour. Add the sifted flour, egg whites and butter to the egg yolks in two lots, very gently folding in each time. Pour the mixture very gently into the tin. To get it into the corners, tip the tin slightly.

Put in the oven and bake for 10–15 minutes. You will know it is cooked because it will be lightly browned and puffed up. When the sponge is cooked, tip it out onto a tea towel dusted with lots of icing sugar. Now roll it up in the towel and leave to cool.

When the sponge is cool, unroll it and spread it with the whipped cream and strawberries, then roll it back up.

SULTANA CAKE

My sister Charlotte is a great cook and this is a cake she often makes.
It is a good balance: not too sweet, yet not so healthy you feel like you
are eating the muesli we used to feed the bulls.

500g sultanas
250g butter
1 cup water
1–2 teaspoons lemon zest
3 eggs
1 cup sugar
⅓ cup brandy
½ teaspoon orange juice
1 teaspoon vanilla essence
½ teaspoon almond essence
2 cups flour
1 teaspoon baking powder

Preheat the oven to 140°C. Line a 22cm round cake tin
with greaseproof paper.

Put the sultanas, butter, water and lemon zest in a
saucepan and bring to the boil. Then simmer for 5
minutes.

Now beat the eggs and sugar until they are thick and then
add the brandy, orange juice and essences. Sift the flour
and baking powder, then alternately add the fruit and
then the flour to the egg mixture, a bit at a time. Pour the
batter into the tin.

Put in the oven and cook for about 1¼ hours. The cake
is cooked when a knife poked into the centre comes out
clean.

Cool in the tin for 10 minutes before turning out onto a
wire rack. It will last for 4–5 days.

BAD-FOR-YOU FUDGE

This has been on our menu from the beginning; we did have a good-for-you fudge, but it was not nearly as popular.

For the ganache
375gm dark chocolate (70% cocoa solids)
125ml cream

For the fudge
250g butter
5 tablespoons honey
4 tablespoons cream
6 tablespoons cocoa
325g plain sweet biscuits, such as wine biscuits
3 cups Chocolate Cake (see page 258)
2 cups ganache

Grease 2 shallow rectangular tins with 1cm high sides.

For the ganache, gently melt the chocolate and cream together in a bowl over a saucepan of boiling water, making sure the bowl does not touch the water.

For the fudge, melt the butter, honey, cream and cocoa together. Then crush the biscuits. Do not crush them perfectly, leave a few large pieces, then add to the melted mixture. Crumble the chocolate cake into the fudge mixture. Then mix it all together well, before pressing it into the tins.

Ice with the ganache and the chill until it is set, 30-35 minutes.

Serve cut into fingers.

Children's Birthday Parties

If you have time it is fun to make some special food for a child's party, but if you don't I am sure your child would much rather you were in a controlled state and would relish just as much all the readymade things you can get from a supermarket or deli. Because, after all, it is your day too; you should be able to relax and celebrate. But if you do have time here are some ideas for recipes that do not take a lot of effort to make.

SAUSAGES ROLLED IN PIZZA DOUGH

Makes 24

24 pure pork or beef
  chipolata sausages
500g Pizza Dough (see page
  88)
1 dessertspoon olive oil

Preheat the oven to 180°C. Grease a baking tray.
Put the sausages on the baking tray and put in the oven for about 10 minutes, or until they are cooked through. You want to just cook them as they will be going back in the oven later.

Increase the oven temperature to 200°C.

When the pizza dough has risen, knock it back and break off bits and roll them into long strips. Now twist these around the sausages, from end to end, and brush them with oil.

Put the rolled sausages back on the tray and cook for 8–10 minutes or until the dough is just lightly brown and sounds hollow when you knock it.

Cool a little on a wire rack, but they are best eaten while still warm.

PIZZA FACES

Makes 8 faces
It is fun to let your children make these themselves. They don't just have to make faces — you could use biscuit cutters and make all sorts of shapes.

400g Pizza Dough (see page 88)
oil
1 cup Pizza Cheese (see page 89)
16 cherry tomatoes
8 pieces salami

Preheat the oven to 250°C.

Pull off 50g pieces of the dough and roll them into balls. Then roll them out into rounds on a floured surface.

Brush with oil and sprinkle over a layer of pizza cheese. Then push the cherry tomatoes into the rounds to make eyes and cut the salami into mouth shapes and put them in the right place. Place on a baking tray.

Put in the oven and cook for 8–10 minutes or until they are golden.

MEATBALLS ON A STICK

Makes 35
This is the same recipe as the meatballs in the meat section, but the method
is different. I would not wait for a party to make these — they are a good
way to get children eating, before they realise they are.

1kg good beef mince
zest of 1½ lemons
¾ cup grated Parmesan
15g chopped parsley
1 egg, lightly beaten
2 slices good white bread,
    soaked in milk and broken
    into little pieces
½ teaspoon salt
½ teaspoon freshly ground
    black pepper

Preheat the oven to 180°C. Grease a baking tray.

Soak 35 ice-cream sticks in water for 30 minutes.

Mix all the ingredients together with your hands until
blended properly. Then pull off clumps and shape
around the top quarter of the sticks. Place the sticks on
the baking tray.

Put in the oven and cook for 20 minutes, or until they are
cooked all the way through.

Serve with Pipi Tomato Sauce (see page 90), or any other
good tomato sauce, and cooked pasta or small bread rolls.

PORCUPINES

Serves 4

This is a meat and rice dish which is great for children and adults. The balls of mince and rice look like porcupines — well, sort of — a good thing to have the night of a birthday party. You don't need to make the Pipi Tomato Sauce; you can use any tomato passata or bought tomato sauce you would use in a pasta dish.

1 cup breadcrumbs, crusts on
1 small onion
4 cups cooked long-grain rice
500g mince
1 egg
½ teaspoon salt
3½ cups Pipi Tomato Sauce
    (see page 90)

Preheat the oven to 180°C.

Blitz the bread and onion in a food processor until it has become tiny crumbs. Put in a bowl and add the rice, mince, egg and salt. Mix it all together well with your hands.

Shape the mixture into balls the size of a small apple and put in an ovenproof dish that fits them all in one layer. Spoon the sauce around and over them.

Put in the oven and cook for 1 hour or until the balls are starting to brown on top and the sauce has gone that lovely deep red it goes when it reduces.

All you need now is some steamed broccoli.

SHAPED BISCUITS WITH STRAWBERRY ICING

Makes 21 smallish shapes
It really is fun making biscuits with children, so get them
to help — the biscuits do not have to be perfect.

For the biscuits

125g butter, softened
½ cup sugar
1 egg
½ teaspoon vanilla essence
1½ cups flour
½ teaspoon baking powder

For the icing

120g icing sugar
1 teaspoon butter
tiny drop of hot water
2 strawberries or raspberries
pebbles and jelly beans to
    decorate

Preheat the oven to 180°C. Line a baking tray with greaseproof paper.

For the biscuits, beat the butter and sugar together until soft and creamy. Add the egg and vanilla and beat for another minute. Then mix the flour and baking powder together and fold into the butter mixture. Bring it together with your hands and knead gently to finish blending it all together to form a ball of dough.

Roll out the biscuit dough on a floured surface until it is about 4mm thick. Cut into shapes with biscuit cutters and place on the baking tray.

Put in the oven and cook for about 10–15 minutes. Take them out and leave to cool a little on the tray before you completely cool them on a wire rack.

For the icing, sift the icing sugar into a bowl, then add the butter and just a tiny drop of hot water to melt the butter. Mash up the berries with a fork to a smooth purée, then add them slowly to the icing sugar until you have a good consistency for spreading.

Let the icing sit for a little while to set and then spread it onto the biscuits. Decorate with pebbles and jelly beans.

REALLY BIG MERINGUES

Makes 8
What is the point of making tiny meringues, when you can make these . . .

8 eggs, separated and at
   room temperature
2 cups caster sugar
1½ teaspoons vinegar
1½ teaspoons vanilla essence
4 teaspoons cornflour

Preheat the oven to 120°C. Line a baking tray with greaseproof paper (wet the bottom to help it stick).

Beat the egg whites until they are stiff, then add the sugar 1 tablespoon at a time and continue beating until stiff.

Next fold in the vinegar, vanilla and cornflour and beat all of this until the mixture is lovely and shiny and mountainous.

Using a big spoon, put about 5–6 spoonfuls on top of each other until you have a big meringue. Repeat and keep doing this until the mixture is all gone.

Put in the oven and after an hour check they are cooked enough — they should be dry and hard — then turn off the oven.

Leave them in the oven until they are dry and perfect, about an hour.

Cream is the best with these meringues, so whip some up and for added effect sandwich pairs together with cream mixed with hundreds and thousands.

ORANGE JELLY BOATS

Makes 12
This is a great way to have jelly and making it out of fruit juice means you can control the sugar levels. You don't have to use orange juice; any fruit juice will do, as long as it is strained well.

3 oranges
2 cups orange juice, strained
½ cup sugar
5 sheets gelatine
¼ cup hot water

Cut the oranges in half and scoop out all the flesh, making sure you do not cut through the skins. Reserve the skins and set aside. Eat the flesh.

Put 1 cup of strained orange juice in a saucepan with the sugar. Heat gently until the sugar has dissolved, stirring all the time.

Mix the gelatine sheets with the hot water and stir until dissolved. Now stir this into the hot juice, then add the remaining cup of strained orange juice.

Put the orange halves on a plate and carefully fill them with the juice, as close to the top as possible. Put in the fridge to set.

Once they are set, you can cut each half in half again.

To make a sail, cut paper into sail shapes. Thread a toothpick through the sail and then stick it in the jelly, and there you have a boat.

PINK LAMINGTONS

Makes 30 small lamingtons
Very pretty, but the jelly traditionally used is not helpful for children's moods. Using raspberries to make them pink leads to a much more civilised party, we hope. First, you have to make a sponge cake. I use a Victoria sponge recipe where you just put everything in a food processor. Queen Victoria had this cake every day for afternoon tea, but I don't imagine she used a food processor. However, we do and it is fine.

For the Victoria sponge
400g flour
400g butter, softened
400g caster sugar
6 eggs
4 tablespoons milk
2 teaspoons baking powder
1 teaspoon vanilla

For the icing
300g raspberries, frozen
800g icing sugar
1½ tablespoons butter,
  softened

2 cups fine desiccated
  coconut

Preheat the oven to 180°C. Line a shallow tin with greaseproof paper. Put all the sponge ingredients in a food processor and blend until just combined. If you need to add more milk then do so; the mixture needs to be slightly runny. Then pour the mixture into the tin.

Put in the oven and cook for 20 minutes or until a skewer inserted in the centre comes out clean. Take out of the oven and leave in the tin for 15 minutes, then turn out onto a wire rack to cool. Now you have the cake, the fun part starts.

For the icing, put the raspberries in a saucepan and slowly heat them through until they are soft. Take them off the heat and add the icing sugar and butter, and mix together well. Now leave to set a little.

Cut the sponge cake into squares. It is up to you how big. For a children's party little ones are good; you will get about 30 small lamingtons from this size cake. Cut off the edges and tops so they are straightish, but they do not have to be all the same size.

Put the raspberry mixture in one bowl and the coconut in another. Dip the squares of cake into the raspberry mixture so they are thoroughly coated on all sides. Then roll them in the coconut, making sure all the surfaces are well covered.

Put on a wire rack to set.

Extras

HERB BUTTERS

We use flavoured butters a lot at Pipi as they are a great way to capture flavour. The method is the same for all of them. Great for melting over vegetables, meat or bread.

Garlic butter
40g parsley
40g garlic, finely chopped
500g butter, softened

Tarragon butter
50g tarragon
500g butter, softened

Orange and thyme butter
10g thyme
zest of 2 oranges
500g butter, softened

Caper butter
zest of 1 lemon
¼ cup capers, finely chopped
500g butter, softened

Put the herbs, if using, in a mortar and pestle and crush them until they are in tiny pieces. Then add the garlic, or zest or capers, and mix everything into the softened butter.

Lay some greaseproof paper on the bench and spoon the butter onto the paper. Now roll it up into a sausage shape, twisting the ends to keep the butter in.

Keep it in the fridge until you need it. When you do want to use the butter, just unwrap and cut off slices in the size you want.

SORREL PESTO

Makes 2 cups
Sorrel is lovely, easy to grow and delicious with fish, as it is very lemony.
This pesto is also great folded through pasta with roast cherry tomatoes.

½ cup pinenuts
4 cups sorrel leaves
⅔ cup Parmesan
½ cup olive oil
½ teaspoon salt
good grind of freshly ground
   black pepper

Toast the pinenuts lightly in a pan. Then put them along with everything else in a blender and whiz.

Pour into a container and cover with a thin layer of olive oil. This will keep for about a week in the fridge.

BASIL PESTO

Makes 2 cups
When basil first comes into season, you have to make this.

4 cups basil leaves, washed
6 cloves garlic, peeled
¾ cup dry-roasted pinenuts
1 cup olive oil
¾ cup grated Parmesan
salt and freshly ground black
   pepper

Pound the basil, garlic, pinenuts and ¼ cup of the oil in a mortar and pestle until you have a fine paste. Add the Parmesan and keep going until it is also completely ground up. Add the rest of the oil and season with salt and pepper to your taste. If you want to make this in a food processor, just follow the same method. Though I always feel that herbs need to be ripped or torn apart rather than cut with a blade.

Cover the pesto with a layer of olive oil and store in a sealed jar in the fridge. It will keep for a week.

SALSA VERDE

Makes 1½ cups
I love this with boiled eggs and new potatoes. At Pipi we put it on the salmon pizza, and sometimes we spread it on a salmon fillet which we then wrap in tin foil and bake in a hot oven. This is a traditional Italian sauce that goes very well with fish, vegetables and roast lamb.

40g parsley, finely chopped
15g basil, finely chopped
20g mint, finely chopped
½ cup olive oil
100g capers, chopped
40g anchovies, finely
    chopped
10g garlic, finely chopped
50g Dijon mustard
2 teaspoons red wine vinegar
salt and freshly ground black
    pepper

Combine everything in a mortar and pestle and grind to a rough paste, or chop it all roughly together on a chopping board.

You can and probably will whiz it in a food processor and that is fine, but I prefer the texture you get when you make it by hand.

The salsa will keep for a week in a sealed jar in the fridge.

MAYONNAISE

Makes 2 cups

4 egg yolks
½ tablespoon mustard
3 tablespoons lemon juice
2 teaspoons caster sugar
1½ cups light olive oil or
vegetable oil
salt and freshly ground black
pepper

Put the egg yolks in a food processor and blitz for a few minutes until they have thickened a little. Now add the mustard, lemon juice and sugar and quickly mix all of this together. Then very slowly add the oil either in a very fine continuous stream or a little bit at a time until it is all combined and the mayonnaise is thick and smooth.

Scrape the mayonnaise out of the food processor bowl and put in a sealed container in the fridge, where it will keep for a week.

DILL AND MINT MAYONNAISE

For the dill and mint mayonnaise to serve with the Whitebait Fritters (see page 166), add ¼ cup of dill and ¼ cup mint to the basic recipe after blending it all together.

LEMON MAYONNAISE

For the lemon mayonnaise to serve with the Poached Chicken (see page 140), add the zest of 1 lemon to the basic recipe.

GREEN CURRY PASTE

Makes 1–1½ cups
There are lots of very good green curry pastes that you can buy, but if you feel like making your own, here is my recipe. If you have the time, it can be very satisfying.

2 shallots

2 stalks lemongrass

3–4 green chillies

9 cloves garlic

good-sized knob fresh ginger, about 7cm long

1 cup fresh basil

1 cup fresh coriander

1 teaspoon ground white pepper

1 teaspoon ground coriander

1 teaspoon ground cumin

4 tablespoons fish sauce

4 tablespoons lime juice

4 teaspoons brown sugar

Put all the ingredients in a food processor and blend until a paste forms. Taste to see if it needs salt. And there it is.

The paste will keep in the fridge for about 2 weeks so you can make a curry easily. It can also be frozen quite successfully.

SLOW-ROASTED TOMATOES

Makes 20
Fresh tomatoes are often disappointing but when you cook them like this,
the change in flavour is incredible. I much prefer them to sundried tomatoes.
The end result should be very flat and rubbery tomatoes, with just a wee
bit of softness left. They have such an intense flavour, they are great for
adding oomph to sauces and stews, or we put them in salads or on pizzas.

10 ripe tomatoes, cut in half
1 teaspoon caster sugar
1 tablespoon olive oil

292 / 293

Preheat the oven to 100°C. Line an ovenproof dish with
greaseproof paper.

Lay the tomatoes on the ovenproof dish, sprinkle with the
caster sugar and drizzle over the oil.

Put in the oven and watch them slowly dehydrate — this
will take about 6 hours. If the oven is too hot to start with,
the tomatoes will release all their moisture at once and will
not dehydrate properly. You may need to experiment with
temperatures as ovens can be different. You can also leave
them overnight in a very low oven.

When they are done, store them in a sealed container in
the fridge with just a drizzle of olive oil over the top. They
will keep for 2 weeks.

CARAMELISED ONIONS

Makes 2 cups
At Pipi we use caramelised onions a lot on our pizzas, but if you have them in the fridge you will find you start using them in and with all sorts of things. Because these are going on the pizzas, you just want the pure onion flavour, sweetened. So this recipe is just pure caramelised onions rather than a jam, which would have vinegar and other flavours added to it.

⅓ cup oil
6 large onions (1.3kg),
    peeled and thinly sliced
5½ tablespoons caster sugar

Heat the oil in a heavy frying pan on a low heat and add the onions. Cover with a lid and, stirring every 5 minutes, slowly soften and brown them. You will need to keep shifting the brown onions on the bottom to the top, mixing them all together, so they get evenly cooked. This will take about 50 minutes.

Add the sugar and cook, covered, for about 10 minutes. Then uncover and cook until the onions are caramelised, about another 35 minutes, stirring often.

This may seem like a bit of a bother, but it is worth it for the smell alone that wafts through the house or, in our case, down Joll Road.

GARLIC CONFIT

Makes 6 bulbs
If you love garlic, then make this. It means at all times you have access to soft,
sweet caramelised garlic. I would spread it on toast or add it to a salad, or soup
or any hummus-type purées. The oil will have become infused with the garlic
so is great for salads or, actually, most things.

6 whole bulbs garlic, washed
1 litre light olive oil

Preheat the oven to 120°C.

Wash and dry the garlic bulbs and put them in an
ovenproof dish. Cover with the oil.

Put in the oven and cook until they are soft and slightly
browned and caramelised. You do not want the oil to ever
come to a full boil, but rather have just a few tiny bubbles
appearing occasionally.

Remove from the oven and when cool, put the garlic and
the cooking oil in a sealed container in the fridge. It will
keep for a week.

BEAN PURÉE

Makes 4 cups
This is a great thing to make when you are sick of hummus. We serve it with our garlic rosemary pizza bread at Pipi. It would also be good with a Greek-style salad. If you have forgotten to soak the beans it's OK, you can used tinned cannellini beans. You will just need to rinse and drain them well and maybe adjust the seasoning a little.

500g dried cannellini beans, soaked overnight
10–12 cloves garlic
juice of 5 or 6 lemons
3 teaspoons salt
2 teaspoons freshly ground black pepper
⅓ cup olive oil

Drain the beans and cook in fresh water until soft, about 1 hour. Drain again and cool. (They will be 1285g wet, so if using canned beans that is the amount you will need.)

Purée the beans with everything else in a food processor until smooth.

CHICKEN STOCK

Makes 2 litres

1kg free-range chicken
    frames
500g free-range chicken
    wings
2 celery stalks
1 onion
1 leek
1 carrot
zest of 1 lemon
2 sprigs of tarragon
small bunch thyme
small bunch parsley
5 bay leaves
8 peppercorns

Put the chicken frames and wings in a saucepan, cover with cold water, and gently bring to the boil. Let it boil away for 10 minutes, skimming the froth from the surface as it collects there.

Now add everything else and let the stock very slowly cook away for 2 hours, continuing to skim off any foam on the surface. It is important the stock does not boil vigorously; the bubbles should just sometimes rise to the surface.

When it is done, strain the stock through a sieve. Let it cool and pour into a container. Store it in the fridge, where it will keep for 2 days, or in the freezer, where it will keep for ages.

Poems

poetry is important, it has always been a big part of pipi, so this book could not be written without including a few.

11 RUNES (FOR ALF, TURNING 11)

— Sam Hunt

1.
I'm not sure what's not
or what's understood:

I'll give what I've got
to see you to manhood.

2.
The sun's on the water.
It's the middle of winter.

I never had a daughter.
Or thoughts of one, either.

3.
This is the way it is:
you're ten, I'm sixty-one.

These (as they say) are
the facts:
we're father and son.

4.
An old friend e-mails:
says she sometimes shakes
her head,

counts the miles; says she
smiles,
surprised, pleased I'm not
dead.

5.
Nikki's right: I'm not dead,
I'm not allowed to die,

not till I'm seventy-seven,
she said.
And no lie.

6.
Meantime, it's solstice,
middle of winter;

'sol in stasis',
sun low on the water.

7.
Alive, Alf, to live
clear of any city;

live as we do, five
gunshots from humanity.

8.
Seems for the first time I'm
close enough up to tune

old words to a rhyme
to tell you the eighth rune.

9.
Three more, too, let's say
a rune a year for the kit!

Let's keep it that way
until one of us can't make it.

10.
When that does happen,
I'll tell you what, Alf,

when the big doors don't
open
and things fall off the shelf

11.
I'll give what I've got
to see you through,

and if I'm not
there, I'll be waiting for you.

SAM HUNT
— AT PIPI

QUEBEC

— Bill Manhire

The café was called Quebec. We used to go there a lot.

The first time, well, we simply liked the name. They had
nothing local, but you could ask for anything else.

In winter they served up hot, brutal stews, which we ate
like soup, using a spoon, and there were rough slabs of
some home-made nutty bread. It was all new to us. In
summer, the desserts were airy, filled with berry fruit, or
made with lemon.

Before it was Quebec, it was Kerouac's. Before that,
I think it was Fettucine, and before that it was a
bookshop, Tom's Exchange. The man who ran it wore a
grey dustcoat. He wasn't Tom. Tom was never there.

This was years before we met. As I recall, the days were
long and awkward. You could take in a few coins and
a couple of old paperbacks, and come back out with
something you hoped might change your life.

ALL DAY BAY

— Barry Saunders

I look at you you
You look around
You look back at me

I look to the ground
Cars go by without making a sound
Words hang in thin air
No one to hear them
Some times I wonder if I'm still breathing
Alone in the world today

Go to some place where no one can find you
Pull off the rope
And any thing that binds you
Untouchable here
Unreachable there
Making songs from the wind
Dreams from thin air
Look down at your shadow
See if you're still there
And just be alone in the world today
Just be alone in the world today.

THE NEW CUISINE

— Chris Price

But excellence had left the old recipes.
It was no longer possible to French dress
for an English audience, or con the locals
with the pallid mash of home tricked out
in fancy language. The chemical gastronomists
had plied their expertise until none of us
would set foot in the kitchen. Even the
traditional dishes had turned sour: milk
UHT, sometimes processed cheese,
faint tang of plastic at the back
of the palate. What all of us once knew
was hoarded in the snowy alpine province
of the few. Time to strike a blow
for – what, exactly? We couldn't say
until that crisp autumn morning when,
after breakfast at the simple wooden
table, Jane picked up a paring knife
as we were thrashing through
the dishes of another dead-end
conversation and thoughtlessly began
her cack-handed, unfamiliar, apt
undressing of the familiar apple.

FOR ALICE HUNT (MY MATERNAL GRANDMOTHER)

— Karlo Mila-Schaaf

remembering
as an adult
that I am still one of Nana's girls
I find myself so lacking

thinking of your satsuma plum
purity
beetroot coloured preserves
rich as raw red livers
nourishing me through otherwise
fruitless winters

you have seen me survive each
christmas
you have seen me eat so many easter
eggs
my body swelling or shrinking
to fit the size of my despair

you have seen boys come in bullrush
madness
and then go
finally
giving me a chance to learn to love
myself

you have seen me dazzling
starry eyed and twirling
at the pinnacle of everyone's
expectations
jubilant

you have seen me under sand
drinking saltwater and hospital
charcoal
the ocean in my eyes
buried beyond hope

you have seen me
when I have not even been there
insanity lingering
and then leaving

you have seen
my fine feathered friends
fleeing the scenes of my crimes
searching for fairer weather

I have made you proud
capping gowns and diligence
rewarded
I have let you down
bounced cheques and bad driving

no matter how far my star has risen
or fallen
you have been as constant as gravity
grounding my reckless heart
without narrowing my horizons

BURIAL WITH FLOWERS

— Ginny Sullivan

It is strange
that anthropologists,
paleontologists,
linguists,
and all those other
heart-numbed specialists
can argue that
those early people
who lived in the dry caves
of the Negev
and along the Dead Sea
could not speak,
only made
rudimentary, gutteral sounds
that are not the noise
of human speech,
when they took their dead,
washed them,
wrapped them in fine red cloth,
and curled them
like infants just born,
their hands clasped on their hearts,
their knees drawn up
into the soft zigzag
of human sleep,
and covered them
with flowers.

ACKNOWLEDGEMENTS

Thank you Jenny Hellen at Random House for taking on this project, and for your excellent guidance and support all the way through.

Brian Culy for capturing so well the essence of Pipi and your unflagging search for the perfect photo. It is three years since Brian and I first discussed a Pipi cookbook.

Leanne Culy's amazing eye for design and grand vision for the project helped to make the whole process one of excitement and discovery.

The poets for their poems and ongoing support.

Nathan and Matt for the photos taken at Greytown Pipi.

Ani Tylee for pushing us forward when we needed it.

Bettina Driscoll for trialling recipes. Cheryl Sucher for excellent advice.

Sophie Phillips for joining us on numerous photo shoots and allowing us to photograph her children.

Selby and Muff Palmer for letting us join your docking team and take photos of your lovely farm.

Bruce Isles and Danelle Dinsdale who have brought the farm where I grew up and graciously allowed us to go back, wander around and take photos (your discreet absence did not go unnoticed).

Also the Pipi cooks who have been called upon numerous times to help, thank you.

POEM CREDITS

'11 Runes (For Alf, Turning 11)' was first published in *Chords & Other Poems*, Craig Potton, 2011.

'Quebec' was first published in *The Victims of Lightning*, Victoria University Press, 2010.

INDEX

almond and cauliflower salad with
    orange dressing 186
anchovies
    and cavolo nero penne 60
    Anchovy, Potato, Taleggio and
        Thyme Pizza 100
    Puttanesca 70
    Salsa Verde 289
apple
    Chicken Confit with Cabbage,
        Cavolo nero and Apple 138
    crumble 218
artichoke, Jerusalem, soup 32
Asparagus, Mint and Lemon
    Pizza 96

bacon
    and blue cheese pasta with
        baby peas 54
    Bloke's Breakfast Pizza 106
    Cabbage, Bacon and
        Mascarpone Penne 58
Bad-for-you Fudge 264
Baked Cheesecake 234–236
Baked Whole Flounder 152
Basil Pesto 288
Basil Pesto with Pasta 72
Bean Purée 295
béchamel (white) sauce 74, 146, 158
beef
    and stout stew 130
    Meatballs on a Stick 272
    Oxtail Stew with Gremolata
        126
    Pipi Meatballs with Penne 64
    Porcupines 274
Big 'Square' Pizza 108
biscuits
    lime and white chocolate 254
    oat 252
    Shaped Biscuits with
        Strawberry Icing 276
Bloke's Breakfast Pizza 106
Braised Lamb Shoulder and
    Kumara Pie 116–118
bread
    Brown Bread Ice-cream 248

Club Sandwiches 198–201
Croissant Bread and Butter
    Pudding 230
Pizza Bread 92
Toasted Flat Breads 204
Pan-fried Toasted Sandwiches
    206
Brown Bread Ice-cream 248
butter, flavoured see Herb
    Butters

cabbage
    Cabbage, Bacon and
        Mascarpone Penne 58
    Chicken Confit with Cabbage,
        Cavolo Nero and Apple 138
cakes
    Bad-for-you Fudge 264
    chocolate 258
    Gingerbread 256
    Pink Lamingtons 282
    sticky date 224
    Strawberry Jam Sponge Roll 260
    Strawberry Shortcake 226
    sultana 262
    Victoria sponge 282
Calamari Pizza 98
Caper Butter 286
Caramel Sauce 224
Caramelised Onion 293
Caramelised Pear, Walnut and
    Rocket Salad 181
Cardamom Pannacotta, Roasted
    Pears and Ginger 240–242
Carrot, Orange and Peanut
    Butter Soup 38
Cauliflower and Almond Salad
    with Orange Dressing 186
cavolo nero
    Anchovy and Cavolo Nero
        Penne 60
    Chicken Confit with Cabbage,
        Cavolo Nero and Apple 138
    Wintergreen Soup 36
celery with poached chicken
    and tarragon mayonnaise club
    sandwiches 198

Champagne and Leek Risotto 48
cheese
    Anchovy, Potato, Taleggio and
        Thyme pizza 100
    Bacon and Blue Cheese Pasta
        with Baby Peas 54
    Cabbage, Bacon and
        Mascarpone Penne 58
    Four Cheese Penne 56
    Gruyère and ham pan-fried
        toasted sandwich 206
    Leek, Mushroom and Goat's
        Cheese Lasagne 74–76
    Margherita Pizza 104
    Parmesan-crumbed Lamb
        Chops 124
    Pizza Cheese 89
    Prosciutto and Ricotta Pizza 102
    Red Wine Risotto with
        Pecorino and Radicchio 46
    Ricotta and hot-smoked salmon
        toasted sandwich 206
    Savoury Scones 182
    Toasted Flatbreads 204
    Watercress, Haloumi and Fig
        and Salad 190
cheesecake, baked 234–236
Cherry Clafoutis 232
chicken
    confit 136
    confit with cabbage, cavolo
        nero and apple 138
    Lemon Roasted Chicken Salad
        188
    Poached Whole Chicken with
        Tarragon 140, 290
    poached chicken, tarragon
        mayonnaise and celery club
        sandwiches 198
    stock 296
Chicken Confit with Cabbage,
    Cavolo Nero and Apple 138
chocolate
    Bad-for-you Fudge 264
    cake 258
    ganache 244, 264
    ice-cream 244

Lime and White Chocolate
    Biscuits 254
Sticky Date Puddings 222
Classic Bellini, 210
Club Sandwiches 198–201
cocktails
    Classic Bellini 210
    Martini 214
    Negroni 212
coffee
    Tiramisu 220
confit
    chicken 136
    Chicken Confit with Cabbage,
        Cavolo Nero and Apple 138
    duck 132–134
    garlic 294
    Garlic Confit Pizza Bread 94
Croissant Bread and Butter
    Pudding 230
curry paste, green 291

dates
    Sticky Date Cake 224
    Sticky Date Puddings 222–224
desserts see puddings; ice-cream
Dill and Mint Mayonnaise 290
dressings
    balsamic vinegar and oil 174
    garlic and walnut oil 184
    hazelnut 68
    mayonnaise see mayonnaise
    orange 186
duck
    confit 132–134
    pappardelle, 66–68

egg
    and ham club sandwiches 200
    Bloke's Breakfast Pizza 106
    Potato Tortilla 170

fennel and kumera bake with
    orange, 172
fig, watercress and haloumi salad,
    190
fish and seafood
    Anchovy and Cavolo Nero
        Penne 60
    Anchovy, Potato, Taleggio and
        Thyme Pizza 100
    Baked Whole Flounder 152

Calamari Pizza 98
Champagne and Leek Risotto
    (with salmon) 48
Fishcakes with Pea and Bean
    Purée 154–156
    stew 158
hot-smoked salmon, sorrel
    and horseradish cream club
    sandwiches 201
Pan-fried Whitebait 166
Salmon Fillet with Rum and
    Lime 164
Salmon Fishcakes 156
Smoked Eel Pâté 202
Smoked Fish and Potato-top
    Pies 160–162
Smoked Fishcakes 156
Quinoa, Tuna and Purple
    Potato Salad 184
tuna, wasabi mayonnaise and
    rocket club sandwiches 200
Whitebait Fritters 166
fishcakes
    salmon 156
    smoked 156
    with Pea and Bean Purée,
        154 156
Four Cheese Penne 56
four spice (quatre-épices) mix 136

garlic
    butter 286
    confit 294
    confit pizza bread 94
ginger
    Cardamom Pannacotta, Roasted
        Pears and Ginger 240
    Gingerbread 256
    Gingerbread Ice-cream 245
gnocchi
    nettle 80
    porcini 80
    Porcini Gnocchi with Sage
        Butter 83
    potato 78–80
    Potato Gnocchi with Tomato
        Ragu, 82
gooseberries
    Fruit Sponge Pudding 238
gravy for roast meat 146
Green Curry Paste 291
Gremolata 128

haloumi, fig and watercress salad
    190
ham
    and egg club sandwiches 200
    Pan-fried Toasted Sandwiches
        206
    Prosciutto and Ricotta Pizza 102
    Vodka, Ham and Baby Pea
        Pasta 52
Herb Butters 286
horseradish cream 201
how to cook
    pasta 52
    pizza 89
    Sunday Roast 146–147

ice-cream
    brown bread 248
    caramel sauce topping 224
    chocolate 244
    chocolate ganache topping 244
    gingerbread 245
    rose petal 246
icings
    chocolate ganache 244
    raspberry 276, 282
    strawberry 276
    white chocolate 254

Jerusalem Artichoke Soup 32

Kumara
    Braised Lamb Shoulder and
        Kumara Pie 116–118
    Kumara, Orange and Fennel
        Bake 172
    mash with orange zest and
        thyme 179

lamb
    Braised Lamb Shoulder and
        Kumara Pie 116–118
    Parmesan-crumbed Lamb
        Chops 124
    shank pie 120–122
    Sunday Roast 146–147
lamingtons 282
leeks
    and champagne risotto 48
    hot, buttered 140
    Mushroom, Leek and Goat's
        Cheese Lasagne 74–76

lemon
    and roasted chicken salad 188
    Asparagus, Mint and Lemon
        Pizza 96
    Gremolata 128
    Lemon Delicious 147
    mayonnaise 290
lime
    Salmon Fillet with Rum and
        Lime 164
    and white chocolate biscuits 254

Margherita Pizza 104
Martini 214
mayonnaise 290
    dill and mint 290
    lemon 290
    tarragon 198
    wasabi 200
meatballs
    on a stick 272
    Porcupines 274
    Pipi Meatballs with Penne 64
meringues 278
mint, lemon and asparagus pizza 96
mushrooms
    and leek and goat's cheese
        lasagne 74–76
    Bloke's Breakfast Pizza 106
    Porcini Gnocchi 80
    Red Wine Risotto with
        Pecorino and Radicchio 46
    Veal with Mushrooms and
        Brandy 114
mustard and sausage penne 62

Negroni 212
Nettle Gnocchi 80

Oat Biscuits 252
onion, caramelised 293
orange
    and thyme butter 286
    Carrot, Orange and Peanut
        Butter Soup 38
    dressing 186
    jelly boats 280
    Kumara Mash with Orange
        Zest and Thyme 179
    Kumara, Orange and Fennel
        Bake 172
Orange Jelly Boats 280

Oxtail Stew with Gremolata
    126–128

pannacotta 240–241
Pan-fried Toasted Sandwiches 206
Pan-fried Whitebait 166
Parmesan-crumbed Lamb Chops
    124
pasta
    Anchovy and Cavolo Nero
        Penne 60
    Bacon and Blue Cheese Pasta
        with Baby Peas 54
    Basil Pesto Pasta 72
    Cabbage, Bacon and
        Mascarpone Penne 58
    Duck Pappardelle 66–68
    Four Cheese Penne 56
    gnocchi see gnocchi
    how to cook 52
    Leek, Mushroom and Goat's
        Cheese Lasagne 74–76
    Pipi Meatballs with Penne 64
    Puttanesca 70
    Sausage and Mustard Penne 62
    Vodka, Ham and Baby Pea
        Penne 52
pastry, short sweet 226
pâté, smoked eel 202
peas
    and bean purée 154–156
    Bacon and Blue Cheese Pasta
        with Baby Peas 54
    Vodka, Ham and Baby Pea
        Penne 52
peanut butter, orange and carrot
    soup 38
pear
    Caramelised Pear, Walnut and
        Rocket Salad 181
    Cardamom Pannacotta, Roasted
        Pears and Ginger 240–242
pesto
    basil 288
    Basil Pesto Pasta 72
    sorrel 288
pies
    braised lamb shoulder and
        kumara 116–118
    lamb shank 120–122
    smoked fish and potato-top
        160–162

Pink Lamingtons 282
Pipi Meatballs with Penne 64
Pipi Pizza Bread 92–94
Pipi Tomato Sauce 90
pizza 85–109
    bread 92–94
    cheese 89
    dough 88–89
    faces 270
    how to cook 89
    Pipi Tomato Sauce 90
poached chicken, tarragon
    mayonnaise and celery club
    sandwiches 198
Poached Whole Chicken with
    Tarragon 140
Porcini Gnocchi 80
    with sage butter 83
Porcupines 274
potato
    Anchovy, Potato, Taleggio and
        Thyme Pizza 100
    Bloke's Breakfast Pizza 106
    Fishcakes with Pea and Bean
        Purée 154 156
    gnocchi 78–80
    gnocchi with tomato ragu 82
    hot, buttered 140
    Potato, Truffle Oil and
        Rosemary Pizza Bread 94
    Smoked Fish and Potato-top
        Pies 160–162
    Quinoa, Tuna and Purple
        Potato Salad 184
    tortilla 170
Prosciutto and Ricotta Pizza 102
puddings see also ice-cream
    Apple Crumble 218
    Baked Cheesecake 234–236
    Caramel Sauce 224
    Cardamom Pannacotta, Roasted
        Pears and Ginger 240–242
    Cherry Clafoutis 232
    croissant bread and butter 230
    fruit sponge 238
    Lemon Delicious 147
    rice 228
    sticky date 222
    Strawberry Shortcake 226
    Tiramisu 220
pumpkin
    Roast Pumpkin and Spicy

Sausage Risotto 42–44
Savoury Scones 182
Spicy Pumpkin Soup 34
Puttanesca 70

Quinoa, Tuna and Purple Potato
    Salad 184

radicchio with red wine and
    pecorino risotto 46
raspberry icing 276, 282
Ratatouille 192
Really Big Meringues 278
Red Wine Risotto with Pecorino
    and Radicchio 46
rice
    pudding 228
    Champagne and Leek Risotto 48
    Red Wine Risotto with
        Pecorino and Radicchio 46
    Roast Pumpkin and Spicy
        Sausage Risotto 42–44
roast, Sunday 146–147
Roast Vegetable Salad 174–176
rocket, walnut and caramelised
    pear salad 181
Rose Petal Ice-cream 246

sage butter with porcini gnocchi 83
salads
    caramelised pear, walnut and
        rocket 134, 181
    cauliflower and almond, with
        orange dressing 186
    dressings see dressings
    lemon roasted chicken 188
    mayonnaise see mayonnaise
    quinoa, tuna and purple potato
        184
    roast vegetable 174–176
    watercress, haloumi and fig
        134, 190
salmon
    Champagne and Leek Risotto
        48
    fillet with rum and lime 164
    fishcakes 156
    hot-smoked salmon, sorrel
        and horseradish cream club
        sandwiches 201
    Pan-fried Toasted Sandwiches
        206

Salsa Verde 289
sauces and spreads
    béchamel sauce 74, 146, 158
    Caramel Sauce 222, 224
    horseradish cream 201
    Pipi Tomato Sauce 90
    Puttanesca 70
    Salsa Verde 289
sausage
    and mustard penne 62
    Big 'Square' Pizza 108
    Bloke's Breakfast Pizza 106
    Roast Pumpkin and Spicy
        Sausage Risotto 42–44
    rolled in pizza dough 268
scones, savoury 182
seafood see fish and seafood
Shaped Biscuits with Strawberry
    Icing 276
Slow-roasted Tomatoes 292
Smoked Eel Pâté 202
Smoked Fish and Potato-top Pies
    160–162
Smoked Fishcakes 156
sorrel
    pesto 288
    hot-smoked salmon, sorrel
        and horseradish cream club
        sandwiches 201
spinach
    bake 180
    purée 180
    Wintergreen Soup 36
sponge, Victoria 238
stew
    beef and stout 130
    fish 158
    oxtail, with gremolata 126–128
Sticky Date Puddings 222–224
Sticky Date Cake 224
strawberry
    icing 276
    jam sponge roll 260
    shortcake 226
Strawberry Jam Sponge Roll 260
Sultana Cake 262
Sunday Roast 146–147

Taleggio, anchovy, potato and
    thyme pizza 100
tarragon
    butter 286

mayonnaise 198
    with poached whole chicken
        with 140
thyme
    Anchovy, Potato, Taleggio and
        Thyme Pizza 100
    Kumara Mash with Orange
        Zest and Thyme 179
Tiramisu 220
Toasted Flat Breads 204
toasted sandwiches, pan-fried
    206
tomato
    Margherita Pizza 104
    Pipi Tomato Sauce 90
    Potato Gnocchi with Tomato
        Ragu 82
    slow-roasted 292
tortilla, potato 170
truffle oil, potato and rosemary
    pizza bread 94
tuna
    Quinoa, Tuna and Purple
        Potato Salad 184
    tuna, wasabi mayonnaise and
        rocket club sandwiches 200

veal
    marsala 112
    Oxtail Stew with Gremolata
        126–128
    with mushrooms and brandy
        114
Vegetable Hash 178
Victoria sponge 282
Vodka, Ham and Baby Pea Penne
    52

walnut, rocket and caramelised
    pear salad 181
wasabi mayonnaise 200
Watercress, Haloumi and Fig
    Salad 190
Wintergreen Soup 36
white (béchamel) sauce 74, 146,
    158, 160
whitebait
    fritters 166
    pan-fried 166